DISCOVERING POTTERY

Published by
Paul Hamlyn Pty. Ltd.
176 South Creek Road,
Dee Why West, NSW 2099
Copyright
Paul Hamlyn Pty. Ltd. 1972
First published 1972
Reprinted 1973
Abridged edition from
The Australian Pottery Book
first published 1970
Printed in Korea
Designed by Bruno Grasswill
ISBN 0 600 07119 7
Jacket photography: Reg Morrison.
Modelled by Trudie Alfred,
pottery teacher at the
Workshop Art Centre, Willoughby.

DISCOVERING POTTERY

harry memmott

paul hamlyn
sydney · london · new york · toronto

contents

preface 7
introduction 8

1. clay 11

Where to Find the Clay 12
The Properties of Clay 12
Plastic. Fillers. Fluxes 16
Equipment for Preparing the Clay 17
Wedging 18
Kneading 20
Drying 22

2. throwing 23

throwing tools and techniques 24

Wheels 24
Tools 28
Making a Bat 31
Techniques of Throwing 32
Problems of Throwing 34
Turning and Finishing 36

throwing actual shapes 40

Throwing a Cylinder 40
Throwing a Large Bowl 46
Throwing a Flat Plate 50
A Cylinder Becomes a Jug 53

3. handbuilding 55

Pinching a Pot 56
Coiling on a Pinched Pot Base 59
Draping a Shape 61
Stoneware Tiles 64
Textured Tiles 66
Handbuilding a Cylinder 68

4. design and decoration 71
Design 72
Slip on Clay 73
Textures Applied to Surfaces 74

5. colour 75
General 76
Vehicles or Mediums for Applying Colour 77
A Guide to Proportions of Oxides for Colour 79

6. glazing 81
General 82
Methods of Applying Glazes 83
Preparing Different Types of Glazes 85
Glaze Faults 92
Glazing a Bottle 94

7. kilns 95
Types of Kilns 96
Preparations for Firing 100
Main Fuels 102
A Simple Gas Kiln 104
A Downdraught Kiln Fired with Town Gas 106
Wood Firing 108
Raku Kilns 111
Kiln Furniture 116
Heat Measurement 116

appendixes 119
index 135

acknowledgements

Without the original teaching by Mervin Feeney this book could not have been written. Most of the throwing techniques illustrated were demonstrated by this 'master of the wheel'.

The section on glazing was collated in co-operation with Milton Moon whose skill in this field is unsurpassed.

Oscar Hausknecht performed feats of gymnastic skill to snap the potter's eye-view of work in progress.

Hours of patient collating and typing, as well as demonstrating were done by Liz Feldman.

Harry Memmott

preface

With the constant search to make our lives fuller, and the awareness that there must be more to life than the popular greed aims of today, pottery, its appreciation and making, has mushroomed in popularity as a means of personal expression.

It is to be hoped that this book will fill a demand for an approach to the art and craft of pottery.

The wheel techniques described herein are those of traditional industrial potters. This knowledge added to, and polished over generations, was about to be lost because of the move of industrial pottery to mass production. Mervin Feeney, a thrower of world standard and trained in these traditions, posed for the throwing sequences. The author, after extensive travels in Australia and abroad, recommends these basic techniques as the most efficient to his knowledge.

Handbuilding, not requiring the intensive discipline of wheel throwing, lends itself to a multitude of techniques and forms, limited only by the experience and imagination of the potter, and the qualities of the clay to be had.

The plasticity of the medium allows a very personal expression of form, only equalled by the unlimited means of decoration. These are attained by the nature of the clay, its textures and colour, the use of its surface for incision or addition; glaze applied heavily or thinly and the effect of firing; the understanding of colour, its contrasts and harmonies.

An added bonus is the adventure of firing, with the knowledge that whatever the potter has done to this point, consciously and deliberately, the fire will now add its comment, perhaps enhancing the work beyond the potter's wildest expectations.

This very complex craft, if successful in all its aspects, then becomes an art. This is recognized in Japan, for instance, to the extent of declaring some potters 'National living treasures'.

Whether or not the reader ever becomes an adept potter, or even touches a piece of clay, this book may help in the understanding of an art to further his appreciation of the art of living.

HM

introduction

This is a book on discipline; the discipline of continued practice, until the article grows of itself, effortlessly and naturally, the mind being in harmony with the forces in use, the material and the design. Unlike some sporting disciplines which create an ability which fades as the body ages, the strength from this discipline will grow and the results will be of ever increasing interest for life.

Hamada, the internationally admired Japanese potter, is about seventy. My grandfather, James Sandison worked until he was past ninety, throwing works on the wheel that young men would find hard to equal in vigour and size. The minds of such men retain youthful zest and inquiry, and their natures reflect the balanced way of their lives. Their way of clay is actually a way of life.

This continuous attempt, along with the mystery of the fire, to capture spontaneous beauty fascinates the imagination, and the mind never grows weary of an adventure which has no ending. But this is only so if there is an understanding, not only of the technique of clay, but of the way of clay. Many promising students show great merit, then fade into oblivion. Having learned the technique, they find they have no knowledge of how to apply their knowledge.

Many students begin pottery with a vague notion of aim. Some have the idea of imitating the most vulgar of commercial pottery. Others are swayed by the most avant-garde of contemporary adventures. However, because of the initial demands of studying technique often their salvation is accomplished as they become aware of the nature of the material, its response to handling, and the subtle glazes of natural materials. Even the most vulgar acquires some taste and the would-be 'advanced' modern gains some depth instead of only superficial showmanship. Technique is the first hurdle. In the case of the potter's wheel, the ultimate quest is to have control of the clay with an ease which allows the mind to deal with the problem of form untroubled by the mechanics of making. This skill is achieved only by long practice, and a sympathy learned of the material and means. The doing can be done without thinking and the thinking is done of the form being made.

Each step of throwing on the potter's wheel will present its difficulties, but no difficulty is greater than the mastery of self. While this is being learned there will be black days of deep despair of ever making anything on this contrary rotating wheel. In some magical way, however, one day the problem will be solved as though the clay itself has suddenly decided to co-operate. The clay is no different, the wheel is the same — could it be the potter?

Sooner or later with practice of throwing, and learning to know the character and limitations of clay, a pot will grow. No worthwhile results will come from strain. Knowledge of using the rigid bones to control the clay and the weight of the body to 'lean on it a little' and guide it on the path of obedience will aid towards ease of making. A touch typist learns to type without looking at the keyboard. Years later she can still type quite well, but without the slightest conscious knowledge of the keyboard. So with the potter's wheel. Having learned the basic techniques, restraint will fall away and the hands will seem to work by themselves. Eventually the potter will be surprised to find that the hands are performing movements as if of their own accord — working out the mechanics of a plan without conscious effort while the design seems to fully occupy the conscious mind.

Technique in handwork is similar. Experience will tell how far a slab of clay will bend, and which joins will remain joined and not crack. Anyone who has seen a native woman animatedly chatting to her friends while she nonchalantly welds coils to make a large jar, will have admired the speed and ease with which she works. The final result is a shape the same as that from the dark past of thousands of years, but the technique is magnificent. A certain quality of aptitude in hand building is necessary to assure ease of making, and confidence the piece will live through drying and firing to allow the mind freedom to consider form.

The mind of the clayworker, if it is to be creative, will of necessity view work from the past, because all art rests upon previous culture. Careful analysis will reveal that even what appears to be the most startling break in tradition is only a rational development from what came before.

While no potter will create original work by merely copying the work of the past, it is still a useful exercise. The purpose of such copying is not to create a slavish imitation but to learn from the problems of construction. That which appears to be straight-forward may be found to be subtle.

Having tried to understand the mind of the mediaeval man who made that jug or the Asian who threw that teapot, and the difficulties they overcame, the next task is to store this knowledge in the reservoir of memory. There it can be used in the attempt to produce a contemporary creation.

Any original work will not be the result of strain, but of a natural and relaxed expression of what has been learned, digested and born as natural of today. Perhaps there may be some strain of body from working with concentration for some time, but if the result is even a little successful this is enough reward.

1. clay

The way of clay is to understand the nature of clay, its wonderful plastic response when handled with love and care, and its collapse and disintegration when maltreated, overworked and strained beyond its capabilities.

Where to find the clay

The problem is to understand where to find it, how to select it, and then to prepare it for its function. If transport and muscles are available, enquiries will usually bring a flood of information about clay deposits. Everybody seems to know of a clay which should be good for making pottery.

Most good clay is some feet under the ground. Places where the earth has been sharply cut into, like cuttings or creek bends, will be where to look.

The properties of clay

What should you look for? The clay may look like clay is supposed to look, a white or red plastic mass, but then it might also be blue, tan, yellow, grey or black. If it is a shale clay, it might even look like rock. Take a small portion of what could be clay, wet it and knead it with the fingers to form a small sausage. Bend it. Try twisting it into a knot. See how far it will bend before it cracks. From this sample an idea of the plasticity can be gained.

The shale type of clay may have to be crushed and soaked for some time before this test can be performed on it. If the test seems satisfactory and sufficient quantities are available to make it worthwhile to use, fill a bucketful and return to the pottery. Lay the clay out in a thin layer and dry it out. Break it into small pieces and add these pieces to water.

Sieve the slurry which has been made through a coarse screen, fine enough to remove objectionable material such as

Examples of short crumbly clay and a fat plastic clay.

small stones, roots, leaves, and so on. Pour the slurry on to a porous surface such as a plaster-of-paris bat, and allow it to stiffen. Now mix or wedge it into a homogeneous mass. This process will be described later in this chapter. Make some shapes which would tend to slump, warp or crack, then make a shrinkage bar. This is a bar of clay about seven inches long, one inch wide and one-eighth of an inch thick. A plastic ruler with millimetres embossed on one side can be cut in halves so that the piece bearing the measure one-to-ten is retained and pressed into the clay bar.

The bar is compared with the ruler as it goes through the various stages of airing, drying and after the biscuit and glaze firings. The approximate shrinkages can then be gauged. Experience indicates that the air drying shrinkage should be about six to seven percent in a throwing clay and less in a hand building clay. The fired shrinkage for stoneware will be about the same.

Plasticity and strength must be considered as two separate qualities. A highly plastic clay may be dug which will assume any shape. But it may have the unfortunate trait of slumping and being unable to support its own weight. Strength may be given to such a clay by adding a fire clay to a sandy type of clay, or any other type of clay which will not only complement the plastic clay and give it strength, but also assist to give the clay body — the remaining characteristics required.

Do not make a clay body any more complex than necessary. Simplicity of ingredients means ease of compounding and more time for making. A simple clay body often has a quality which is lost in a complicated formula. The finer and denser the clay, the greater the difficulty of drying, and the more likelihood of warping and cracking. Most of these problems can be overcome with the addition of *grog* (ground firebrick of various mesh size) obtainable from a supplier of refractory products. The problem is to balance the non-plastic qualities of grog with the desirable high plasticity of the clay. Many potters prefer to add a sandy open clay which has some plasticity, to grog, which has none.

When stoneware pottery is fired and is required to *vitrify* (become glass-like) enabling it to hold fluids, even if unglazed, it must have a porosity of less than five percent. If the clay body, on its own, will not achieve this result the potter must add *flux* — that is material such as feldspar which fuses the clay particles. Feldspar is the most common ingredient used in the clay body as a flux, dissolving first the clay particles then the silica as the temperature rises, and forming the body into a vitreous mass. It is also a non-plastic in the clay body. Its purpose is to give vitrification and strength. Too much of it of course will cause deformation, warping and excessive shrinkage. The fired colour of the clay is controlled by the oxides in the clay, usually iron. Additions of other oxides and minerals can alter the colour as required.

Clay gathered locally gives the potter an awareness of the close relationship of earth and pottery.

Bought clay, highly refined by wholesale suppliers, is usually characterless. All the faults and impurities which give a clay personality have been removed. But, if a reliable, refined, powdered clay is available, the method of making a clay body is the same as with dug clay. Some character may be added to it with a rougher body, such as fire clay.

The three main constituents of a clay body are: plastics, fillers and fluxes. Plasticity is given by the clay and will vary greatly with different clays. Fillers open the clay body, allow drying, and reduce shrinkage and warping. They are non-plastic. Fluxes cause the body to fuse into a solid mass and mature at a given temperature. Fluxes also act as fillers during air drying. The selection, and quantity of these materials, will depend on the type of ware to be made and the temperature at which it will be fired.

Plastics

Kaolin or China Clay has low plasticity and dry strength. It has small shrinkage and is *refractory* (hard to melt).
Ball Clays are used for plasticity. They are fine grained and have a high dry strength. On their own they shrink excessively.
Stoneware Clays have similar plasticity, but greater refractory characteristics.
Fire Clays are refractory, some types are strong and plastic and very useful in a throwing body. They will assist with any drying problems.
Bentonite is very fine grained clay used in small quantities (about one or two percent) to give plasticity.

Fillers

Silica, sand, quartz or flint are non-plastic. They open the clay body to assist in drying and reduce shrinkage and thus prevent cracking. During the firing they act as 'bones' to the piece giving it strength to retain its form without slumping, or reducing fired shrinkage.
Grog, crushed fired ceramic, has the same purpose.

Fluxes

Feldspar, the most common flux, melts to bond the body together when fired.
Nepheline-syenite fuses at a slightly lower temperature.
Limestone (whiting) and *talc* are sometimes of use.

    A throwing clay will be highly plastic and strong with emphasis on ball clay and fire clay for these qualities. For hand work and tiles the clay will need to be much more open and greater stress will be placed on fire clay and fillers. *Casting slip* (liquid clay for casting) will need less plastic qualities and kaolin and fillers will dominate.

Equipment for preparing the clay

It is possible to buy fully prepared clay from a pottery supplier, or the local pottery or brick works. These days large potteries usually run their clay through a de-airing pugmill. This mixes the clay and removes the air from it by means of a vacuum chamber. This has the effect of making a clay of very even and plastic quality, requiring only kneading before use. If such a supply is available it will be a blessing.

If the clay has been *pugged* (mixed) in an ordinary pugmill, it is desirable to allow it to age for several weeks, before it will gain the qualities that a de-airing pugmill provides. After ageing it is better to knead or wedge the clay by hand rather than to pug it again.

The importance of maturing clay may be judged by the great care which some Asian potters take to prepare clay for use by future generations. They are working with clay that their grandfathers prepared for them. The hand or foot wedging of clay is a process with obscure origins. The resulting smooth even body is only equalled by the de-airing pugmill of comparatively recent times. The process drives the air from the clay and mixes it to a homogeneous mass. It also reveals any foreign bodies that may have worked into the body of the clay.

After the clay has been wedged twenty-one times it has over a million cuts through it, and becomes of even appearance and nature. Watch the surface of the cuts each time, and remove any foreign bodies that may have got into the clay.

Cut at least twenty-one times. After the trouble of wedging, do not allow the clay to deteriorate by lying it flat on any surface. Stand it on an edge so that the smallest part possible is touching. When the clay is cut up for use leave the last thin strip on the table, as it will be uneven in texture after losing some of its moisture to the surface on which it was resting.

The potter's tactile and visual senses will tell him when the clay is just right for use.

When the clay has been wedged and has lain around for a while it may become crusty — the outside stiff and the inside soft. Kneading is used to recondition the clay to an even condition.

Wedging

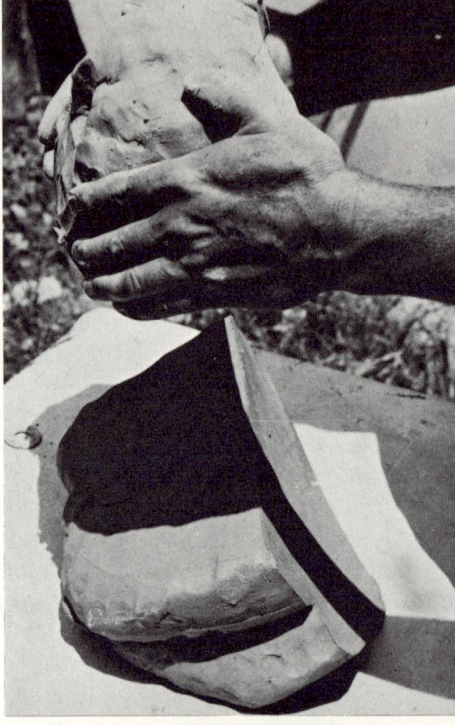

1   Working on a damp plaster block or table beat the clay into a shape as shown. Resting it against the body, raise it enough to pass the wire under and vertically up through it.

2   Place the cut ends towards the body and grasp one half of the clay with the palms rather than the fingers.

3   Swing the clay high and, using its own weight for momentum, strike it forcibly downwards on to the half on the wedging block.

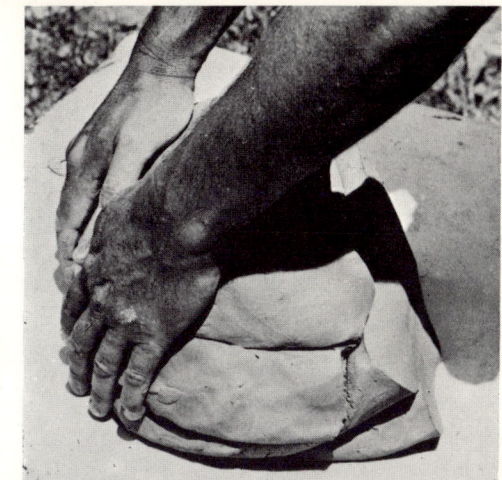

4   Push the hands and fingers forward on the clay to the block.

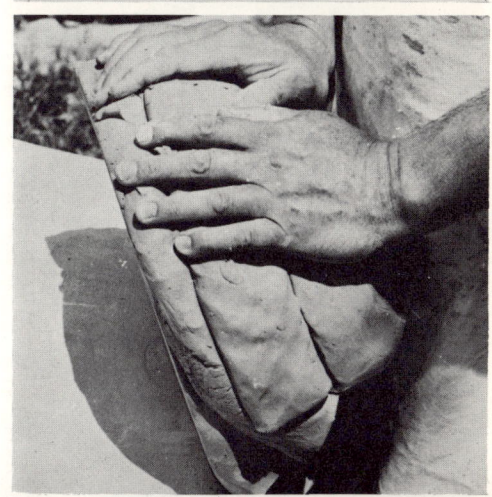

5   Pushing the hands forward causes suction which allows the clay to be lifted towards the body.

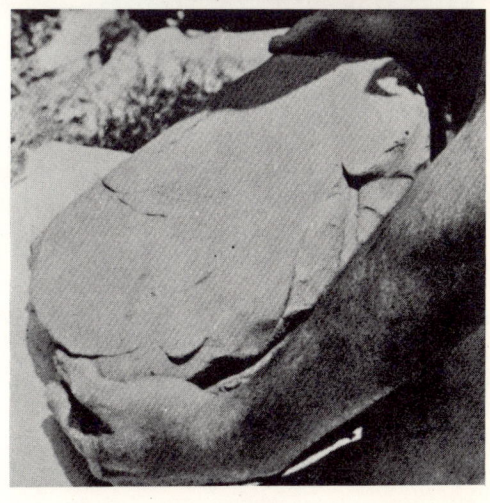

6   Then turn the clay away from the body with the left hand, while your right hand moves towards the body. The clay is now back in its original position looking like a capital D, ready for the next cut and a repetition of the movements. Use the palm of the fingers to beat it into shape if necessary, and run the fingers over any surface cracks or marks. Cut and wedge at least twenty-one times.

Kneading

 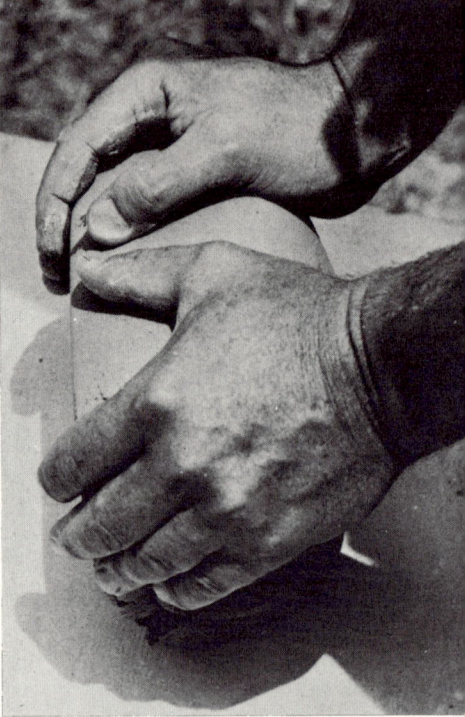

1 The clay is placed on a plaster block. Kneading is done to freshen up a piece of clay which has been standing for some time after wedging.

2 Hold the hands as illustrated and lean the body weight onto the clay while continually rotating the clay towards the body for a quarter of its circumference at a time.

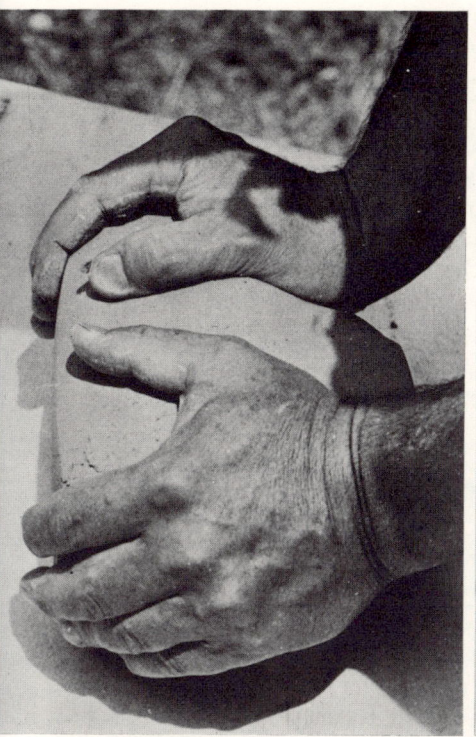 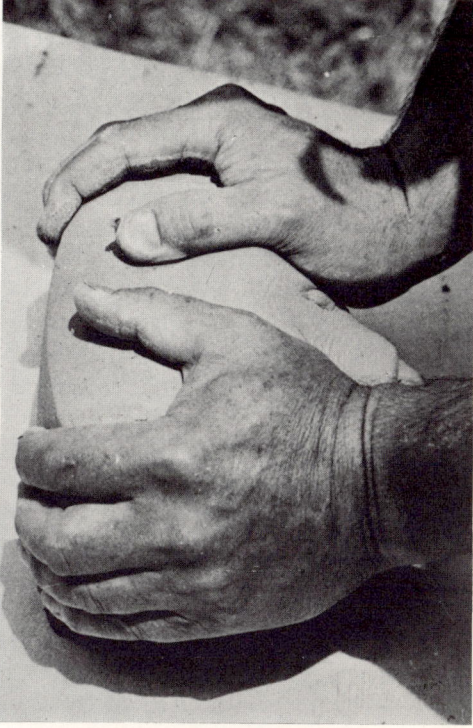

3   Press down with the heels of the hands while keeping the fingers at the ends of the clay to prevent spreading.

4   As kneading progresses the clay will assume the appearance of a ram's head. By eventually reducing the pressure of the hands, the clay will revert to the rolled shape. Stand the clay on its end upon the block, and tap and rotate it to form a ball for throwing.

Drying

Most ceramic pieces are lost during the air drying of the ware. Generally this is caused by a lack of understanding of the process plus the use of excessive water when making.

Shrinkage, the cause of cracking, is equal in volume to that of the water evaporated. If the clay is saturated, particularly at the base which is always the slowest portion to dry, this is an invitation to cracking. Remove a piece off a wet bat as soon as possible and place it on a dry absorbent surface. Coarse-grained clay, like some kaolins and fire clays, shrinks less than fine-grained ball clays. The coarse grains, or grog added to clay, allow the water to escape into the atmosphere. Fine plastic clays retain water. As the ware dries at the surface, the inside remains wet and the resultant strain causes cracking.

The potter has no option but to proceed carefully and slowly unless artificial means of drying are available. This is particularly true with large pieces. The larger the piece, the more non-plastics will probably be needed in the body.

The main drying problems are preventing the fine portions of the ware from drying too quickly (such as handles on jugs), and speeding up the slow drying parts (such as the base). The portions required to dry slowly may be wrapped in plastic. The slow parts can be dried by standing them on very absorbent surfaces or open mesh. As soon as possible the piece can be stood upside down or laid on its side.

Warping may occur during drying because of strain incurred during making, negligent handling, or uneven drying. The circular mouths of the ware can be kept round by using specially made forms, or old cracked bowls to dry on. Ensure that the curve of the piece used as a support is not too acute because the drying piece may shrink on to it causing cracking.

Bowl shapes can be cupped mouth-to-mouth to retain their shape. Air or sun can be a problem, causing distortion on one surface. When bowls are drying upside down the base tends to rise. If the base is convex, this makes the bowls into a top, or a 'spinner'. While the clay is still plastic, paddle it down slightly in the centre of the base and avoid this trouble. Certain shapes may be found impossible to dry. The only answer is to alter the shape or to add non-plastics.

2. throwing

throwing tools and techniques

Throwing on a potter's wheel is an art which the professional craftsman fully understands. The means and materials used are always the best available. A beginner will have enough problems throwing, without trying to use a wheel which has a jerky motion, or which wobbles from an insecure frame or light material structure.

Wheels

A wheel should be chosen for its smooth running. It should have enough force or momentum to prevent the braking actions of throwing from stopping it easily. It should be built heavily enough to prevent it vibrating. Its driving mechanism and bearings should be big enough to keep it running evenly. Its speed should be about 0 to 150 revolutions a minute.

Some throwers favour *kick wheels* — that is wheels propelled by the foot. Kick wheels are certainly the easiest and cheapest to make and maintain. As the thrower has to provide the driving force, it is as well to be sure that kicking is not beyond the physical capacity of the person who is going to use it. In places where a ready-made wheel is available, price it first to see if it is really worthwhile making one.

Kick wheels can easily be made by a handyman. The frame, drive shaft and bearings should be heavy enough to assure stability. The flywheel runs well if it weighs about 100 to 112 pounds. Rust proof materials are desirable for the tray. It must be built firmly enough to brace the forearms against without a feeling of insecurity. It should be rounded on the edge for comfort. The seat, if one is used, should be about level with the wheel and sloping slightly forward.

It is possible to convert the kick wheel into a power wheel by several methods. One which causes engineers to shudder, but which works well, is by the use of a slipping pulley belt. In

1 A kick wheel.

these days of trade-ins, most of the parts required can be cannibalized from old washing machines. A long drive belt will be needed, and even a round industrial sewing machine belt will do, but a V belt is better. By the tension applied to this belt, the wheel can be driven at variable speed. Many other methods are used, but the beginner should do very well with one man power.

Construction of a power wheel always has the problem of how to obtain variable speed. One answer is friction wheels, where a small diameter wheel moves on the radius of a large wheel. Variable speed pulleys, cones which move and run one against the other, patent clutch devices, hydraulic controls, electrical controls, and other devices can also be used but many of these are very expensive. One of the cheaper methods to use is the variable speed pulley. For any type of wheel a quarter to half horsepower motor is sufficient.

Hydraulic and electrical variable speed devices incorporated with the motor are available, but these are expensive. Most of the wheels in use in our pottery are of an old fashioned heavy industrial type, using a leather friction wheel passing over a larger wheel radially to vary the speed. Wheels using this principle will work very well as long as they are not too light. Small bearings and fragile friction wheels will not last long. It would be wise to obtain advice from a practising potter before buying a wheel.

Any light should be over, but slightly in front of the thrower to avoid working in one's own shadow. All switches should be waterproof, as a thrower's hands are always wet and covered with clay slush.

2   Electric potter's wheel (studio type). (Courtesy: Production Brazing Company P/L)

Tools

Throwing tools can be made from the simplest materials. To make a cutting needle sharpen a meat skewer, stick it through a cork, grind it to a fine point, and it is ready to use with a ring to hang it up by.

A wire cutter can be made with nylon fishing line, or piano wire tied to two bamboo nodules, washers, or whatever is handy.

Flat tools can be shaped from wood, metal or plastic. Flexible ones can be cut from shim steel, brass or rubber.

Turning tools can be made from hoop iron and sharpened, or from wire or thin fret saws formed into a loop.

Sponges will be necessary. Flat sea sponges are useful for throwing. Cheap plastic ones are best for cleaning up. A sponge

1   Inside and outside calipers for measurement of diameters.

tied to a stick is needed to remove any water that may remain in deep cylinders where the hand cannot reach.

Calipers, inside and outside, are obtainable from hardware stores. Do not buy the type which screws up. The screw fills with clay and water, and soon will not work.

A small piece of leather or material is handy to round the rim. It will also quite easily become part of a pot if it is left lying around, and becomes attached to other clay.

For cleaning the wheel and bats a paint scraper is perfect. When throwing, the view of the potter is restricted almost to a plan view. An old mirror set behind the wheel will give a profile view.

2 These wooden tools have varied uses for finishing work.

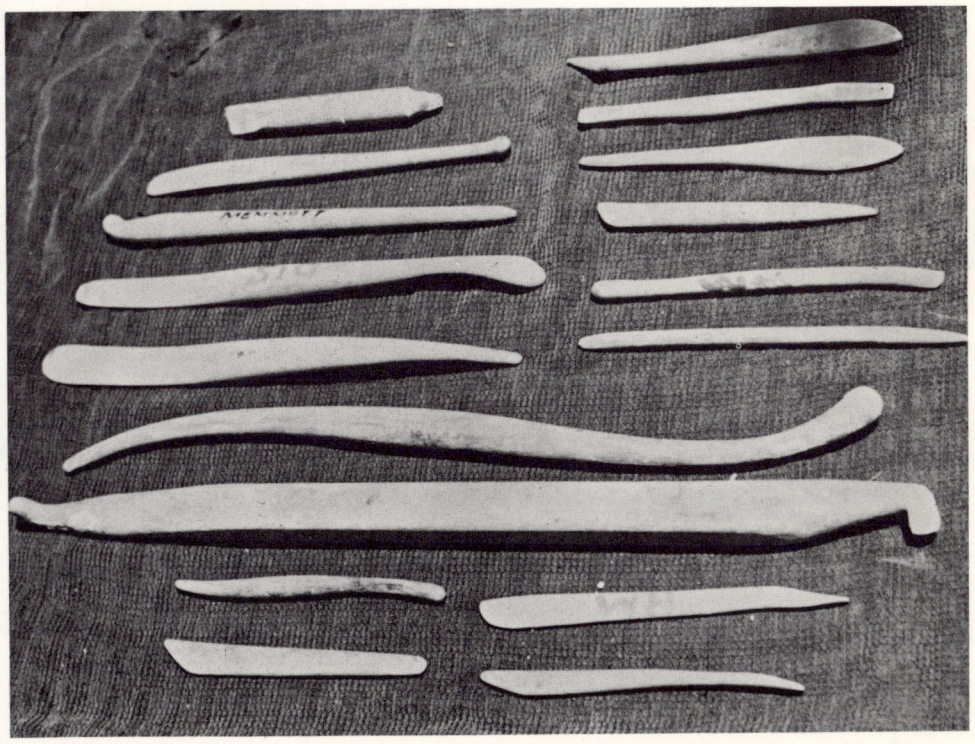

3 Turning tools.
4 Various throwing implements.

5 Knives, tools for making holes and a scraper.

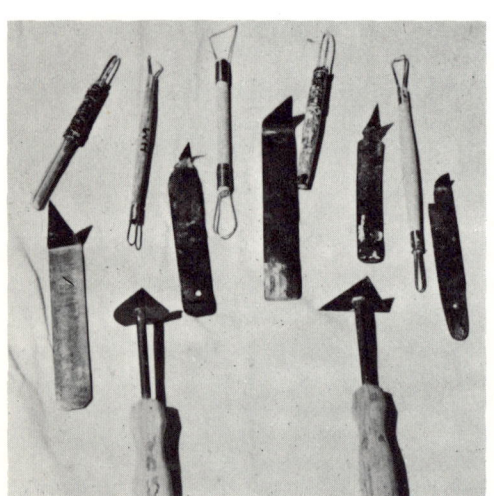
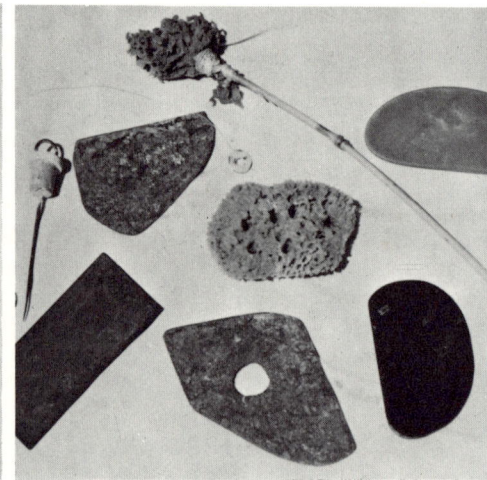

Making a bat

Wide diameter pieces are difficult to remove from the wheel head without distortion. Circular bats of some material are needed. Asbestos cement pieces, usually thrown away by builders, may be cut to a circular shape and used. A circle of clay is thrown on the wheel, and as long as it is wet enough to supply suction, the bats will stick to it. The bats should be slightly moistened so that they will not dry the clay circle hard, preventing adhesion. If the bat is too absorbent waterproofing may be necessary.

1 A circlet of clay is thrown to hold the bat.

2 The bat is placed on the clay circlet. A smear of clay is put on the bat to hold the piece.

Techniques of throwing

A bowl of water will be needed on the right side of the wheel. The soupier the water is with clay slush, the better lubricant it is, and the less likely to cause cracking in the clay. A good plan is to consider a throwing programme some days ahead if special clay is required. Very soft clay can be used to throw wide, flat plates. Firmer clay will be necessary for tall work. Thick ware should be well grogged.

With supreme optimism, the beginner will select clay to use with absolute disregard to its use or condition. Watch an experienced thrower carefully select the clay and then spend time preparing it to a perfect condition by wedging or kneading, after which the clay ball is shaped without flaws and of the correct weight for the size to be thrown.

Wedging not only removes the air from the clay it also seems to make it more plastic. No lumps, cracks or crusty surfaces are acceptable in the ball of clay about to be thrown. The ball of clay should be circular, with its ends flattened, something like a cheese. A crease left in the clay ball may remain on the pot bottom, creating a flaw which will develop into a crack later. Only sufficient clay balls should be made for immediate use, because the clay condition deteriorates quickly forming a crust on the outer surface. There should be no water or wet clay on either the clay ball or the wheel head as this will prevent adhesion.

Prepare the surface of the wheel to accept the clay ball by smearing some clay on it. The residue left when a pot has been cut and removed from the wheel is ideal to throw on. Under no circumstances throw the clay on a dry, dusty or wet, slushy wheel. In both cases, the surface may reject the clay ball and send it flying.

Adherence to the wheel is best obtained if the clay is thrown on to a moving wheel. If the clay lands off centre, stop the wheel, and try again or simply push the clay into the centre.

One school of potters in Japan has for many years deliberately thrown eccentrically off centre to give an individual character to their ware. This is a quality so many people, taught to accept uniformity and mathematical balance, are at a loss to appreciate. Before attempting to imitate such esoteric styles, however, the beginner would be advised to learn full control over the medium. The forces involved in centring must be considered. If the clay is moved towards the centre, centrifugal force will hold it there. As it moves outwards, the same force will throw it off the wheel. A fast speed will assist in centring, this same speed continued when the piece grows larger will probably cause its destruction.

A cone can be made on the wheel, with the wheel travelling at high speed. But if you pull the rim out to form a bowl at this speed, the result will be disastrous. It is most important to bear this in mind all the time. A fast wheel speed is best for centring gradually reducing as the pot nears completion. Large diameter bowls will be finished at the slowest speed commensurate with throwing.

There are different approaches to centring, but one thing all experienced potters have in common is that the clay is not pushed symmetrically to the centre. The arms must be braced, and held in a rigid manner to command the conduct of the clay. If the hands are moving from side to side during centring, the clay is the master and the thrower should stop and consider how to achieve authority over the clay. Rest the forearms on the side of the splash tray, or brace the elbows into the sides of the body.

One method of centring is to push the clay away from the body with the heel of the left hand against the movement of the wheel, while the fingers of the right hand are used to pull the ball of clay towards the body. A larger ball of clay may be easier to centre if you extend you left hand past the centre of the wheel, and directly away from your body, while your right hand braces your left and shapes the ball of clay.

Squeezing the clay so that it rises up and then pushing the ball down again will improve its condition if repeated a few times. Some throwers centre the clay into a high conical mass and then force the hand to open it up.

A good style is to centre the ball about one and a half times as wide as it is high. This allows the base to be finished immediately by pressing the thumbs down into the centre of the clay until the correct thickness of the base is reached. Use a needle to ascertain the correct thickness if necessary. Do not plunge the needle into the centre of the base but to one side. The centre is harder to heal. Experience will soon make this test unnecessary.

Problems of throwing

The beginner's way can be thorny. Even an experienced thrower has periods of error when nothing will go right. Here are some of the common troubles which most beginners encounter.
1. The beginner has an optimistic attitude that any clay in any condition is suitable to throw with. Only a skilled thrower can competently handle short or weak clay, and would never throw with clay improperly wedged or kneaded. The beginner blissfully ignores that which the expert insists upon.
2. Do not use excessive weight of clay to attempt a shape. Throw with the minimum amount of clay to improve technique.
3. Correct centring is essential for symmetrical work. In normal throwing the clay must be truly centred in the early stages of throwing.
4. Cracking is usually caused by the use of too much water. Lubricate the hands with clay slurry rather than water. Do not throw water on the pot. Do not allow water to form a pool inside the pot.
5. Remember to brace the arms rigidly when centring. If the hands are moving in an erratic way, the clay is in control — not the thrower.
6. Use slow rhythmic movements of the hands. Do not release the hands from the pot abruptly. Drawing up the walls too quickly in relation to the speed of the wheel will also spiral the wall and make the rim uneven.
7. Keep even pressure on the walls while drawing up. Usually the inside and outside pressures are applied opposite one another, however when drawing up, the outside hand can be under the inside.
8. Do not be too long in making the basic shape. Clay suffers from fatigue and will collapse.

9. Control the top edge constantly. Keep the rim thick until the completion of the shaping. This will give the rim strength and stability.
10. Do not make a shape which will slump either just after making or during the firing.
11. Join the thrown accessories such as handles and spouts as soon as possible. Do not forget to trim the body of the pot if it is too heavy.
12. Allow for firing shrinkages and glaze thicknesses. If a lid has to fit into a neck, there are several layers of glaze to contend with.
13. Consider the relationship of the body to the wheel before starting. Do not place yourself in an awkward position. Have all the necessary tools and materials to hand. Be above the wheel if possible.
14. When cutting the pot off the wheel head, keep the wire down hard on the wheel. Cut away from the body.
15. Use the needle to test the thickness of the base. Try to keep the base and the bottom of the wall thin, and retain clay near the rim to be used as the pot develops.
16. When drawing clay out on the wheel to form a flat plate, do not take it too far and cause a collapse as the clay supply runs out. Stop before this happens and draw up the sides.
17. If a tool is being used, make sure that it is done to maximum advantage. For instance, a flexible tool should fit the curve, not just touch a segment of it. A needle should be held rigidly when trimming a rim. Be precise when using calipers and make sure the measurement is as it should be. Do not make a lid too large or too small to fit the bowl through faulty measurement.
18. Finally but most importantly the thrower's approach should be one of total empathy with the piece at hand. The body should not be in a condition of locked rigidity, too stiff to even move, or have the sloppiness of a body without bones. It should be braced to force the clay's obedience without losing the fluidity of movement, or becoming tired from tension. A clear idea of intent should be held, with a plan of the sequence of movements needed to make the piece.

Turning and Finishing

1 When turning a wide, flat shape on the wheel, it will probably not need to be supported.

2 Special chucks may be used for pieces to be placed over or in for turning.

3 A block of clay thrown on the wheel can form any of these chucks. A cheese-cloth cover will prevent adherence.

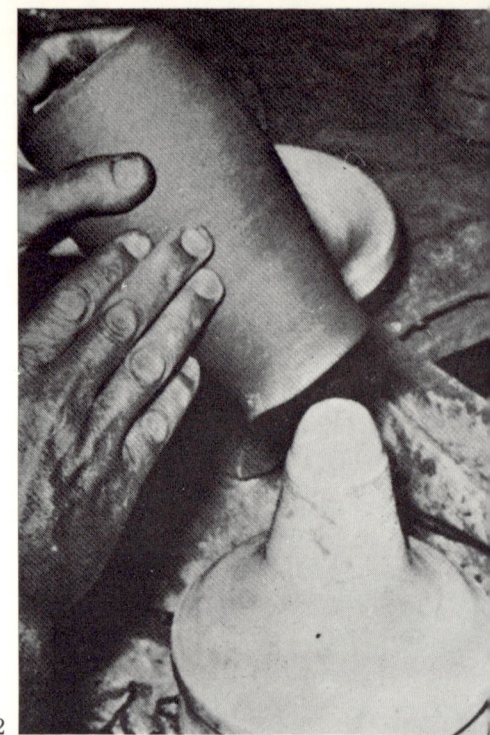

37

After a pot has been thrown, it may be necessary to thin its walls.

The piece is allowed to harden, care being taken that it is not exposed to air or heat unevenly so that one side will dry more than the other. When the clay is of a heavy cheeselike consistency, and strong enough to be handled, it is known as leather-hard. This degree of stiffness for turning will vary. A large flat plate will have to be quite stiff, or it will flop while handling. A bowl which needs to have a handle attached or to be beaten into a shape will be much softer. The ideal state for this process is when the clay peels off in long even rinds.

Various tools are used. They include loops of wire or fine saw blades on a handle, metal hooks made from hoop iron or ready made tools from the suppliers. Brass tools are useless for this process because they will wear too quickly. Fine fret saw blades bent round and onto a handle and then bound are efficient and cheap. Flat tools must be kept sharp. Turning can be done on the normal head of a potter's wheel as in the following illustrations.

Practice will be needed, so keep all pots initially for turning practice. When in doubt as to whether the pot is centred, hold a finger near the edge. If the distance between the rotating pot and the finger remains even, then the piece is running true, if not, the pot is either not centred or out of shape. If one part of the pot is definitely out of line with another decide which will be accepted, and centre the piece with this portion running truly. The wheel should travel at a good speed. The tools must be sharp and rigid. A selection of files will be necessary for sharpening, as the clay blunts edges quickly.

Hold the turning tool firmly with a braced arm. Do not follow the surface of the piece. The tool should slowly approach the wall, taking off high spots and only then begin to turn the main wall of the pot. If the piece is not quite circular, after turning for a while and then stopping the wheel, it should be possible to observe that the high spots are being cut into, and the low spots are untouched. If this does not happen, the tool is being held too loosely and the hand is being controlled by the uneven surface. It is best to aim at throwing pots which do not need turning. This is most unlikely to be possible for some time, but mastery of the clay will never be gained if the thrower depends on turning.

Some pots will be deliberately thrown thickly to facilitate the shaping of the pot in planes, ridges or other designs, or making shapes virtually impossible by normal even throwing.

The base of the pot is usually left flat in stoneware. Practice should make it unnecessary to turn, although a hit with a paddle on the centre of the base will make sure the piece sits firmly. Some potters use a twisted cutting wire (usually made by plaiting three strands together) to cut the pot from the wheel head, leaving a characteristic pattern on the base of the pot. If a foot is desired, that is a ring of clay on the base, a little extra clay is left when throwing to allow for this to be turned. When turning a shape where it is impossible to feel the thickness of the clay to check it, tapping the surface and becoming used to the sound and feel will give the answer. Where the body is of coarse ingredients and a smooth surface is required, a soft kidney-shaped rubber is used, this will press the surface smooth. A sponge removes the fine and exposes the coarse particles so making the surface rougher. A flat steel edge on a fairly dry surface will expose the grog and cause cavities to give a rough finish.

Many potters use slip to brush on or dip the ware into, to give smooth finishes which are often coloured. This is a matter of taste, and the piece itself should suggest whether it needs a smooth or rough surface. Check any pieces which must fit. Lids will have shrunk slightly faster than the main body but if, when thrown, a lid was on the large size, now is the time to shave a trifle from it. Turning must be done in sympathy with the clay. A shape may be turned from a live thing into a hard mechanical nonentity. When a pot is turned it tends to lose the character of direct throwing. The appearance is of tool cutting, not the softer surface more subtly made by the fingers. Even the feel of the pot is different. Examine the shape carefully. Let it speak. Do not dictate to it.

throwing actual shapes

Throwing a cylinder

The cylinder is the greatest challenge to the would-be potter on the wheel. Much practice is necessary to persuade the clay to defy gravity, grow slowly higher and yet to keep the walls evenly thin. Here it is demonstrated by a professional potter with quick precise movements perfected from years of practice.

Speed is essential when making a piece of height, as after a time the clay becomes fatigued from an excess of handling which causes the sides to slump, and the cylinder to lose height.

1 The ball of clay is centred, with the ball being about one-and-a-half times as wide as it is high.

2 The thumbs are pushed into the centre of the clay and pointed slightly towards the body. The arms are braced rigidly on the side of the wheel tray or against the sides of the body. The hands surround the clay and the right thumb pushes towards the little finger of the right hand while the left hand steadies.

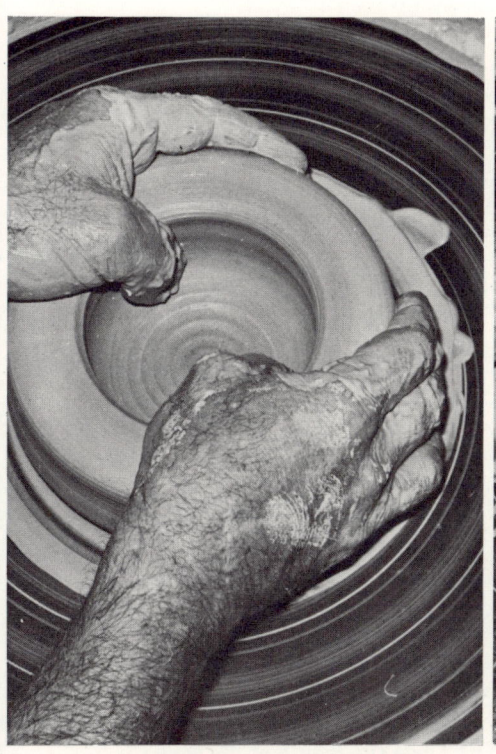 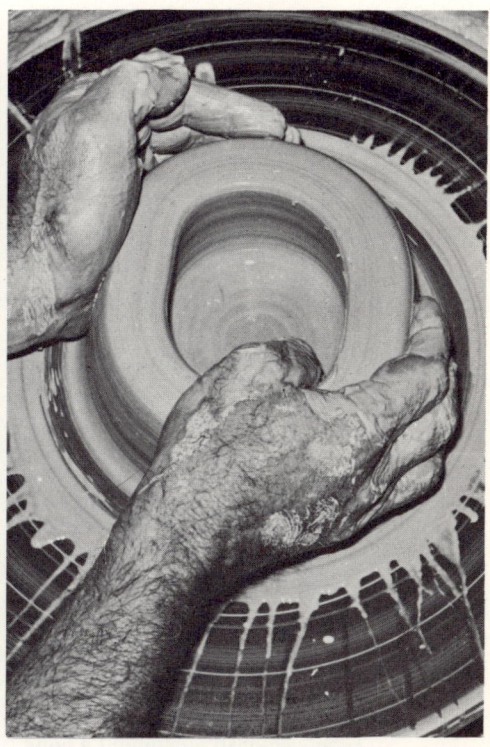

3 A bowl shape develops. Widen the bottom making sure it is the correct thickness. Test with a needle if unsure.

4 The outside is gathered to the approximate diameter of the base. The bottom is now slightly larger in diameter than it will be when finished. Now think of the clay as if it were a stick that is being picked up with the thumbs back towards the little fingers for a start, and ending up opposite the centre of the hand.

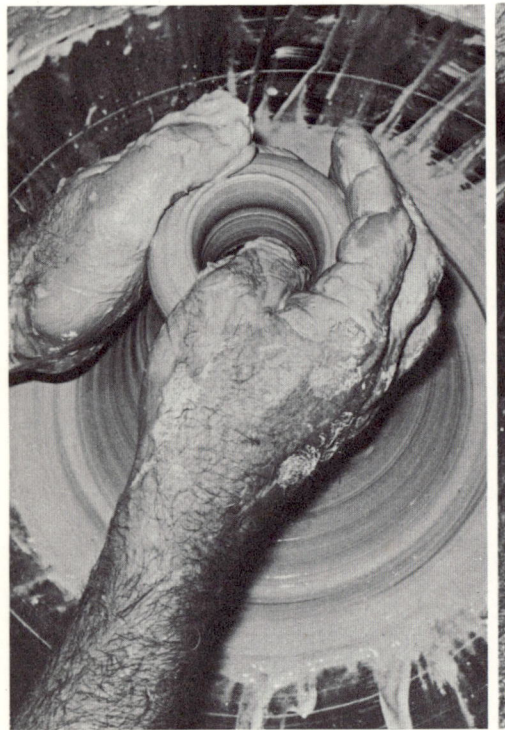 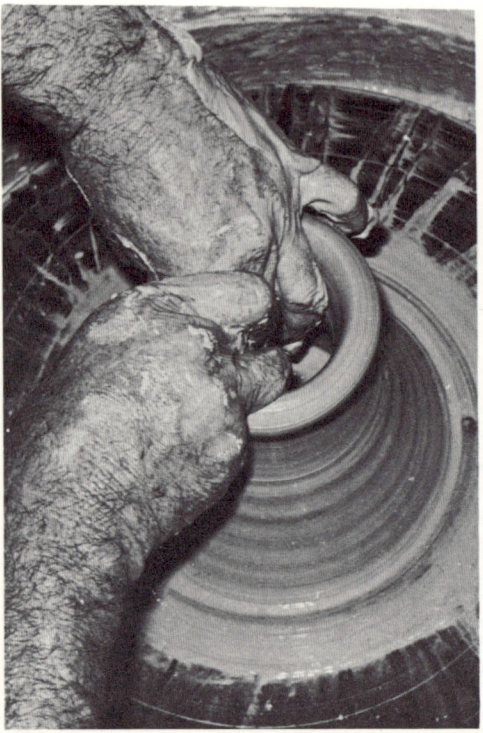

5 In one smooth movement a cone is drawn up. Put pressure on with the thumb, and with the heel of the left hand pressing towards the centre of the wheel, the clay rises to a conical shape.

6 Open the mouth of the cone to permit a hand to fit inside by putting two or three fingers of the hand into the mouth of the piece. Let the clay run up between the small finger of the right hand and the second smallest finger, right up to the knuckles as shown. Let the clay run up between the thumb and the forefinger of the left hand, and steady the clay as the mouth is opened.

7 It is worked up again to required thickness. The middle finger of the left hand, being the longest, will go to the bottom of the cylinder. Then with the right index finger braced with the other finger and thumb try to feel through the bottom wall of the cylinder for the finger pressing out from the inside.

The left thumb is used to brace against the knuckle of the right forefinger. The clay is now allowed to ride up steadily. Keep the mouth of the cylinder narrow. The wider it gets, the less control there is over the clay. Try to draw the clay as high and narrow as possible.

8 The piece is not quite a cylinder yet, it is hollow in the centre, slightly wider at the top and still wide at the bottom, with the bottom walls still a little thick.

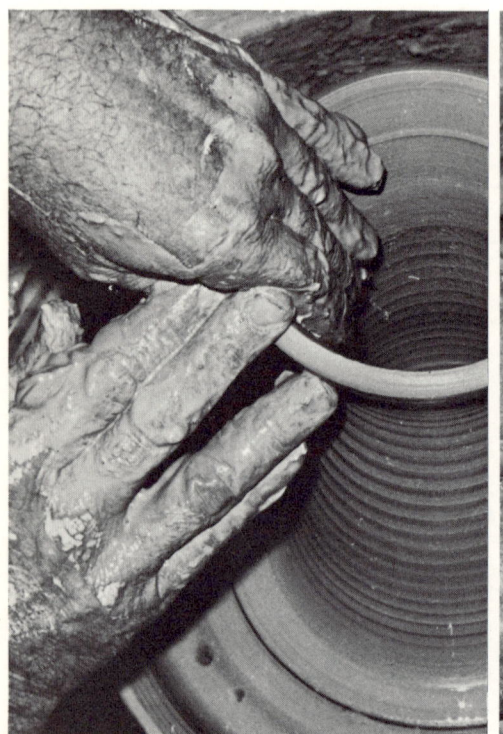 

9 The rim is steadied. The fingers of the left hand are inside the cylinder, the thumb outside. The middle finger of the right hand is on top of the rim, the second smallest finger pressing slightly on the outside. Do not let the top of the rim run dry. Only dampen the hands, do not throw water on the clay.

10 The excess clay is removed from the base. As there is slightly too much clay at the bottom of the cylinder, remove it now with the finger or a tool.

11 A final drawing up removes the lipped shape of the rim and it becomes a true cylinder. Put the left hand down as far as possible into the cylinder feeling through with the middle finger of the left hand from the inside and the fingers of the right hand from the outside. Press again, keeping a little more pressure on the right hand than on the left hand, otherwise the cylinder will get too wide, and as the aim is height not width, keep it narrow. Do not try to lift all the clay from the bottom with one lift, this will weaken the clay. Try to lift two or three times.

12 Here in the final stage the rim is trued.

Throwing a large bowl

1   Throwing large pieces requires skill and strength. The technique is to use the hands rather than the fingers. Here the thrower has centred a piece of clay about ten pounds in weight, and has made it about four inches high.

2   The heel of the left hand is forced into the clay with the arm very stiff, and the right hand steadying with the fingers on the outside of the clay. Note how the arms are bracing one another, and a strong clean rim is kept on the clay.

3   The ball of clay has been hollowed out, and as soon as the thickness of the bottom is established, the clay is forced outwards to slightly more than the finished width of the bottom (the right hand should steady the left throughout this part).
   The clay is then gathered inwards to the approximate finished diameter of the base.

4 With one smooth movement the clay is lifted up into a cone twelve or fourteen inches high.
   Both hands then grip the top rim firming and truing the clay, making the mouth of the cone wide enough to admit the right hand.

5 The excess clay near the base at the wheelhead is removed, and pressure is applied radially inwards.

6 The right hand is now placed inside, and the left outside, applying pressure almost evenly from both sides.

7   The shape is drawn up and the top is narrowed.

8   The position of the hands is now reversed. The left hand is inside and the right outside. More pressure is being exerted outwards than inwards, as further height and shape are developed.

9   The shape is refined and trued.

Throwing a flat plate

1   In this instance centre a ball of clay about three pounds weight so that when centred it measures about six-and-a-half inches in diameter and about one-and-a-quarter inches high. This is achieved by pressing the edge of the right hand down on the top of the ball of clay to flatten it, whilst keeping the left hand pressure slightly on the outside of the clay ball, stopping it moving out of true, and giving the required shape.

2   The grip is now changed and the heel of the left hand is pressed on the centre of the clay, the arm being quite straight, braced from the shoulder. Steady with the tips of the right fingers, pressing down to flatten the clay. At the same time let it go outwards, bending the tips of the left fingers into the edge to stop wobbling. Continue this movement until you have a flat pancake of clay on the wheel, of a thickness near that desired.

 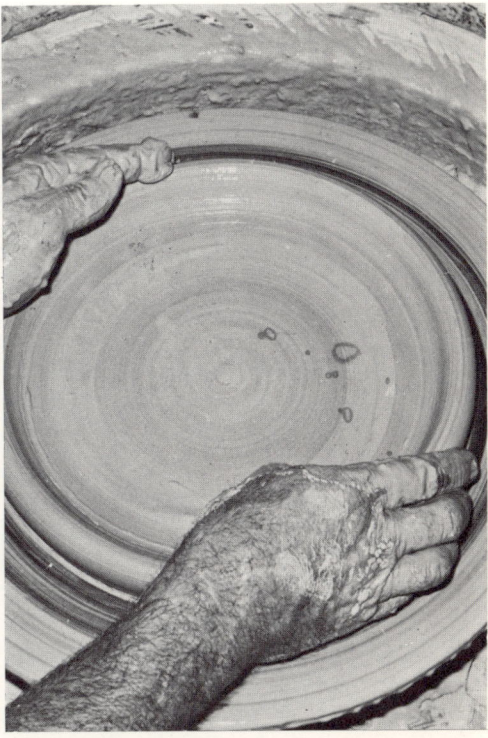

3 To gather the edge, the hands are placed on the outside edge of the clay, the thumbs on top. Pressing with both small fingers towards the centre of the wheel, gather the clay and turn the edges up.

4 Remove the 'rag' of clay on the outside of the piece against the wheel, using the tip of the finger or a tool. This possibly eliminates the need to turn the foot.

5   Curving the outside edge. Bring the tips of the middle and second and smallest fingers of the left hand inside the rim, pressing outwards slightly against the support of the right index finger, curving the side into the required shape. Keep the thumb of the right hand on the edge to keep it true.

A cylinder becomes a jug

Throw a cylinder as described. A spout is then worked into the cylinder. One way of doing this is shown here.

 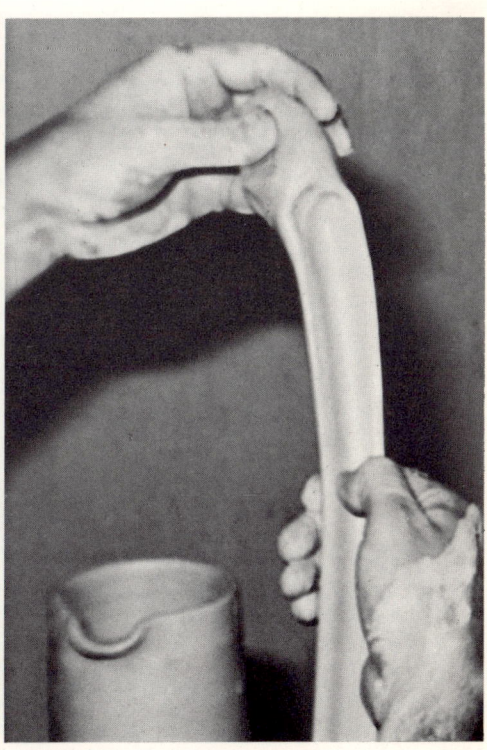

1 The index finger of the left hand supports under the spout. The thumb is placed at the side of the spout, whilst the wet right fore-finger forms the spout. The hands are then changed over so that the same process is repeated, but with the opposite hands.

2 A handle is then pulled and attached to the form.

3 The jug is now finished.

3. handbuilding

Pinching a pot

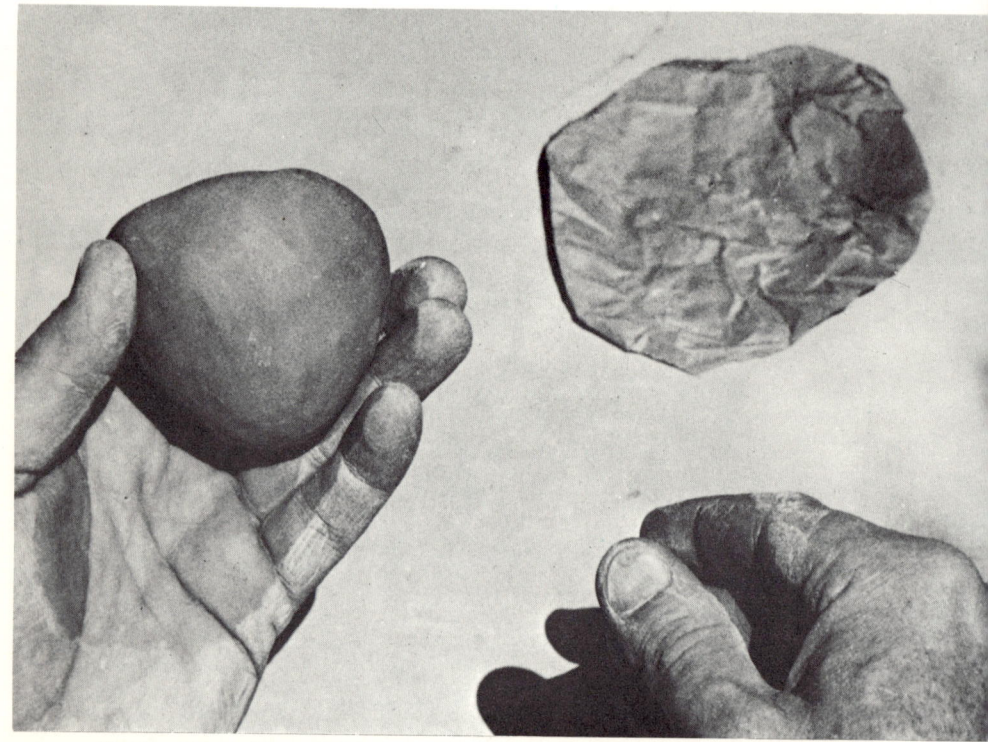

During the making of this little pot, the hands should be kept clean and slightly moist. Dry hands, especially with dry clay on them, absorb the moisture from the clay causing it to crack.

1   Take a small ball of clay which will easily fit into the palm of the left hand, and a piece of paper about two inches in diameter. Slightly cone the ball of clay and flatten one end making sure the surface is smooth and without any flaws.

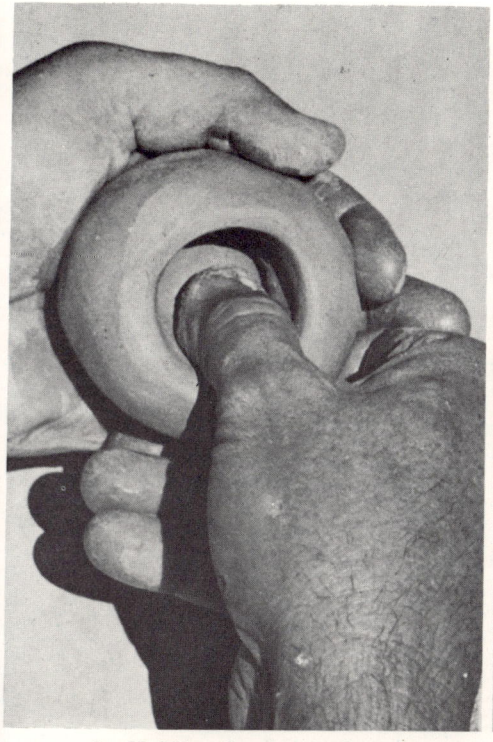 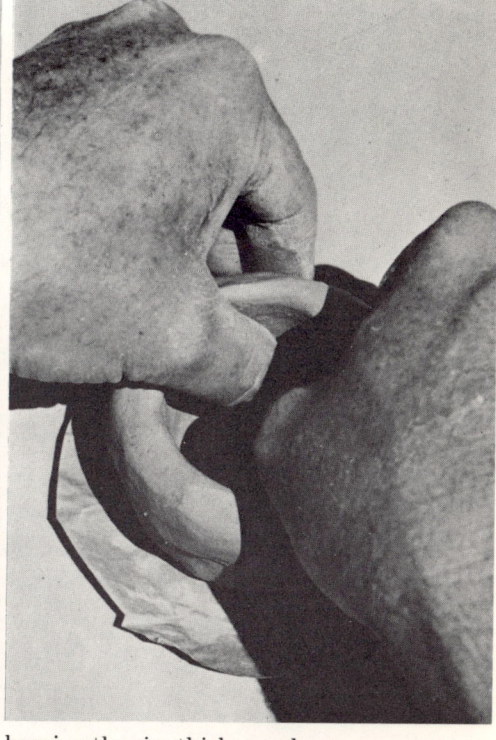

2 Holding the clay in the left hand, press the right thumb into the flat end of the ball of clay. Turn it continually in the left hand. Do this until the bottom is almost the correct thickness and the ball is opened out sufficiently to allow for freedom for the thumb and fingers.

3 Next place the little bowl on the piece of paper, gently flattening the base on it. The piece of paper will act as a bat allowing the clay to be freely rotated on the table whilst thinning the wall. Concentrate working round the foot of the pot keeping the rim thicker and rounded, making sure that no cracks appear. If they do, rub them out with a slightly moistened finger.

As the pot is opened out, two hands may be used, continually pinching the walls thinner and causing them to rise higher and higher whilst at the same time rotating the pot so that attention is given to every section of the wall. The rim is thinned last, and trimmed if desired. This process is continued until the wall is tidied. Throughout making, the pot may be picked up and rotated in the left hand if this will allow easier access to the walls and the base.

4 The pot is now finished. The Japanese made tea ceremony bowls in this way. This method can be used to make any open vessels and the size depends on the capabilities of the potter. A bowl made in this way acts as an excellent base upon which to build a coil piece.

Coiling on a pinched pot base

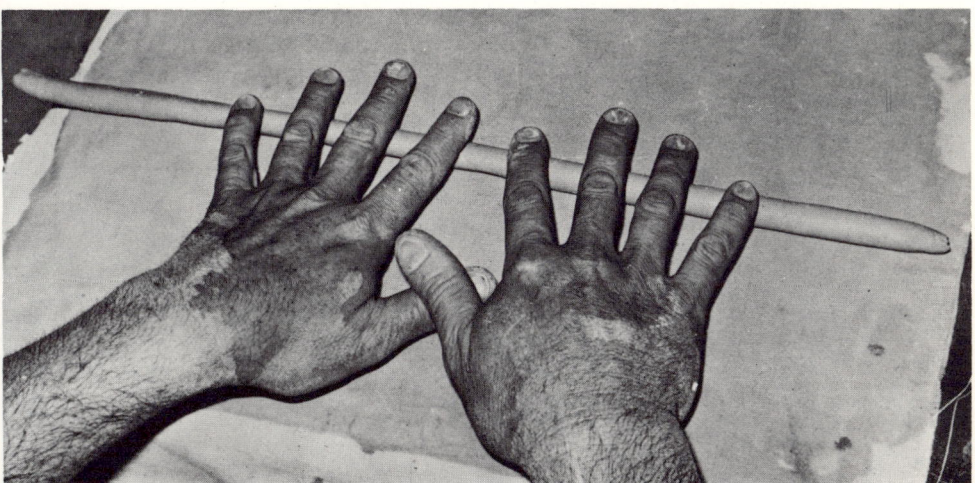

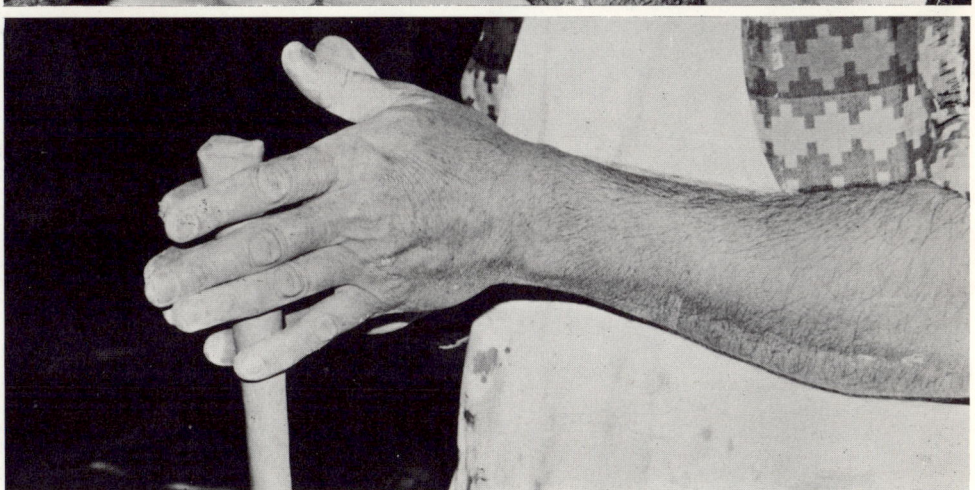

1 Roll the clay horizontally with fingers spread apart, rotating the clay to its full diameter.

2 The clay can be rolled vertically, but this requires more skill.

3   Join the rolled coils to the top edge of a pinch pot with a downward pressure of the thumb. The wrist is then rotated to allow the forefinger to press down and inwards on the outside. Further height can be quickly gained to make tall objects, although some time may have to be allowed at stages, for the walls to stiffen to support the extra weight.

Draping a shape

1 A clay form is made on which to drape a slab of clay. It is supported off the bat to leave room for trimming. Cheese-cloth is wrapped around the form to prevent the clay sticking.

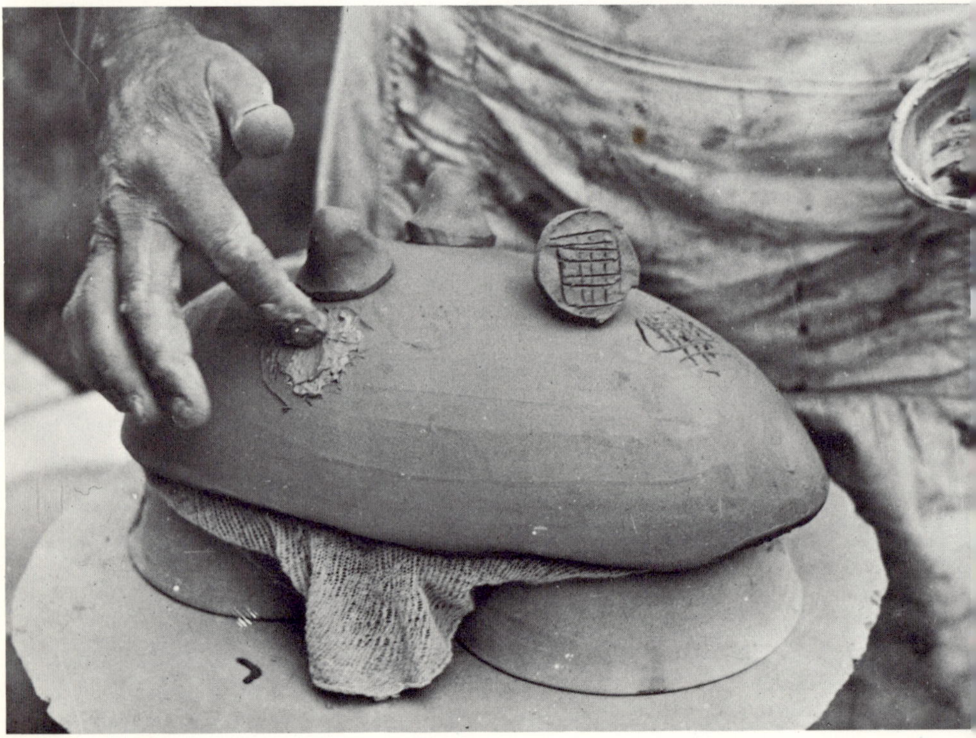

2   A slab of clay is cut and laid over the form. With a damp, flexible tool the clay is persuasively shaped to assume the contour of the form. Excess clay is removed from the rim as the process continues. The rim is them trimmed.

3   Three feet can be modelled and placed on the shape to see how they will look. A flat bat placed upon them will show if they are going to support the shape evenly. Mark the position of the feet. Then score the feet and the surface to which they will be adhered. Thick slip is used to join them firmly to the shape. A surface pattern may be added.

4   The bowl is removed from the mould form as soon as possible after it stiffens. If it is left too long it will shrink onto the mould and crack. The rim can be made level by rubbing it on an even wet coarse surface.

Stoneware tiles

Stoneware tiles have a distinctive character. They look hard and strong — and they are. But the glaze can be soft, deep and lustrous. The restrained colour of stoneware glaze makes this type of tile harmonious with any modern interior decoration.

A table tiled with stoneware tiles is a simple but impressive project. Ample grog should be used in the clay, up to thirty percent may be used. Allowance should be made for shrinkage, so that a tile measuring six inches by six inches will probably be made six-and-three-quarter inches by six-and-three-quarter inches. Only a shrinkage test will give this, if it is important. In any case, it is wise to have the table made after the tiles are made, then you can be sure of accurate fitting.

The tools required to make tiles are a length of canvas or some similar material, cutting wire, a needle, a large palette knife, two strips of wood about half an inch thick, a rubber mallet, some cheese-cloth or muslin, a paint scraper, a small steel straight edge, a bag of silica and a pattern of the tile in its preshrunk size. A number of pieces of asbestos cement wall board slightly larger than the tile size will be required to dry the tiles between.

1 Prepare the clay, well grogged and fairly stiff. Wedge and thump it into a suitable shape. Place a piece of canvas on the table to stop the clay from sticking. Place two half inch wooden strips each side of the clay and guide the cutting wire by these strips as you pull it through the clay to give an even slab.

2 Place the tile pattern on the clay. Keeping the needle vertical, cut around the pattern, remove any 'rags' which might be around the edge.

3 Any small marks can be removed with a paint scraper. Sandwich the clay tile between two pieces of asbestos cement to dry. You can place tiles four high between alternating squares of asbestos cement. Do not put them higher than this because the weight will crack the bottom tile. Turn the tiles upside down several times while they are drying, but keep them between the asbestos cement because this assures even drying on both sides of the tile and prevents warping. When the tile is dry it can be sandpapered along the edges and fired.

Textured tiles

The making of tiles presents many possibilities of design to the potter. On flat tiles interesting effects can be created with glaze, using the glaze to convey the design. Again the potter may be preoccupied with textures and surface contrasts, or three dimensional concepts. Tiles can be used for mass effect or spot decoration. Their surface may be smooth for functional purposes, such as a table top. They may be made in the deepest of relief for decorative purposes.

Tiles with textural surfaces are easy to make and can be used in many ways. Any form can be impressed into the clay to create a design on the tile.

1 Cut a well-grogged piece of clay about half an inch thick. Take a length of muslin and cover the clay. In this illustration an unusual weathered piece of limestone is used to impress a pattern on the clay with a rolling action.

2 When the cloth is removed, the pattern is revealed.

3 Cut the tiles into their planned sizes and place them between asbestos cement sheets to dry. Tiles of different designs can be placed together for the top of a coffee table.

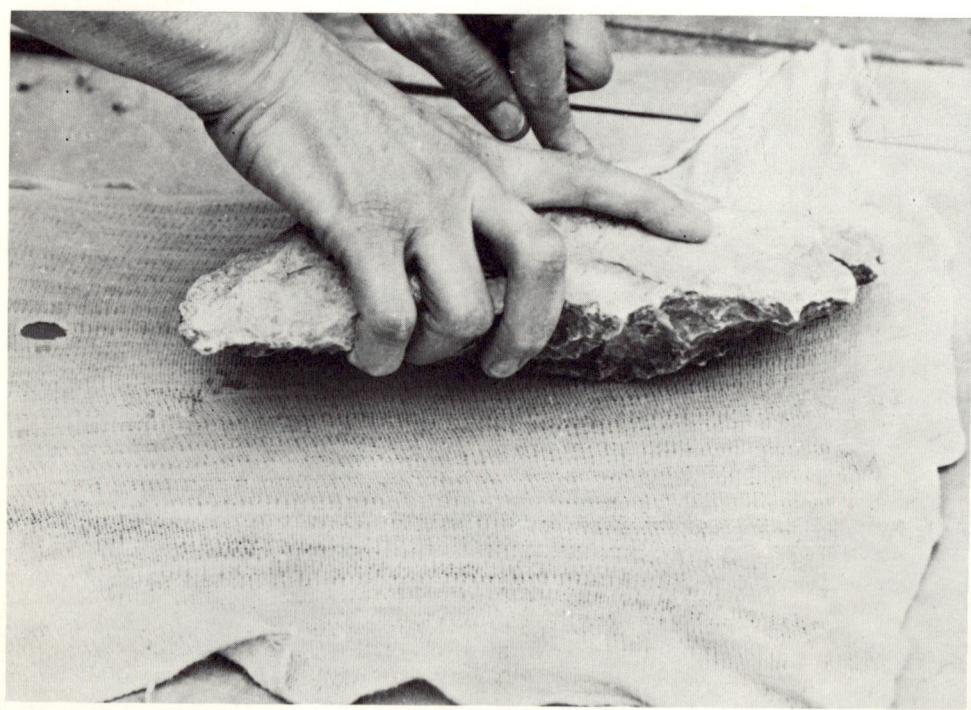

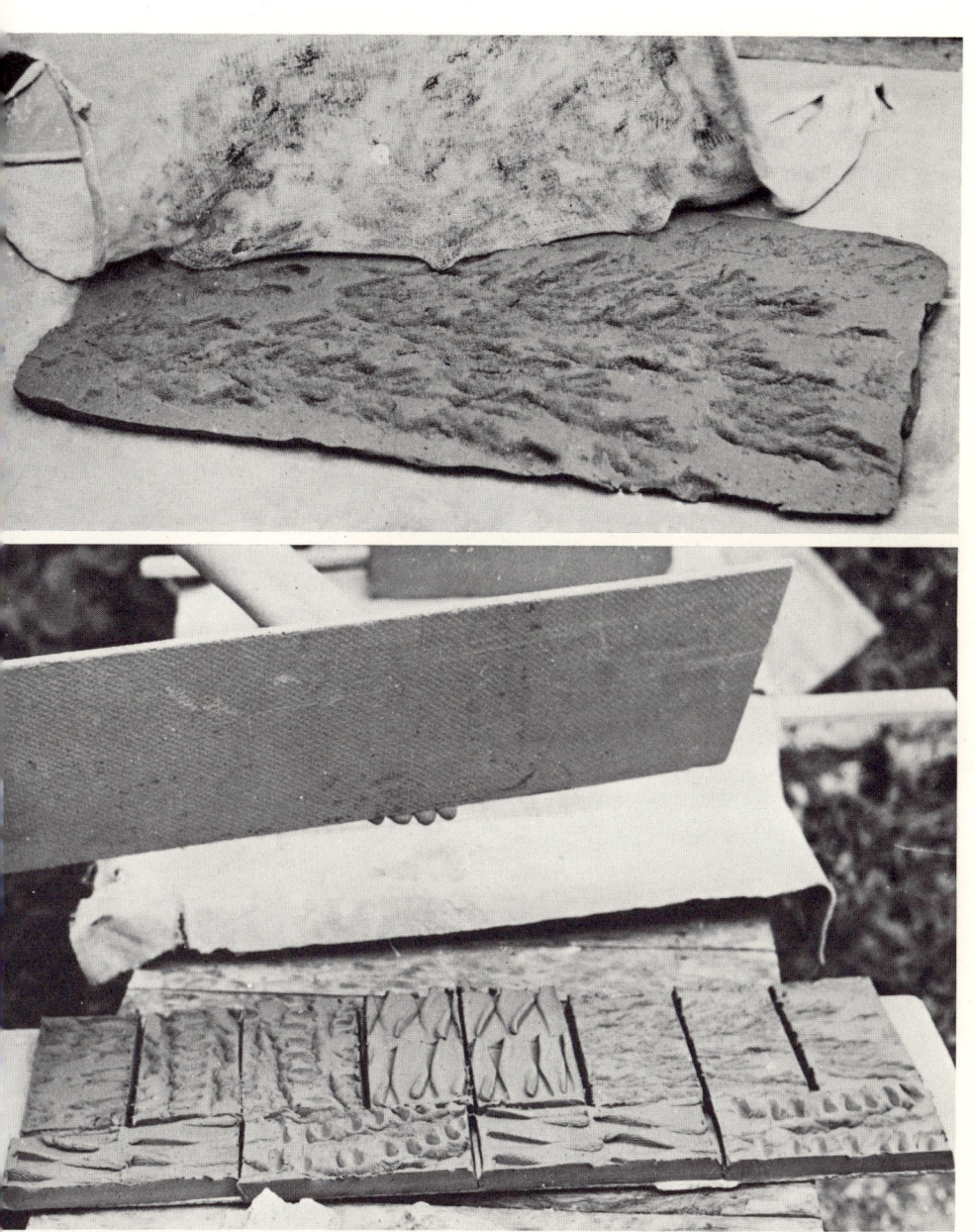

Handbuilding a cylinder

Many ways of combining various means of making will become apparent with practice. A simple cylinder can be used as it is made, shaped as shown, beaten into oval or squared shapes, or combined with other forms.

1 Wrap a cardboard cylinder in newspaper. Keep one end of the newspaper flush with an end of the cylinder. Roll a slab of clay onto the cylinder. Keep one edge of the clay slab flush with an edge of the cylinder.

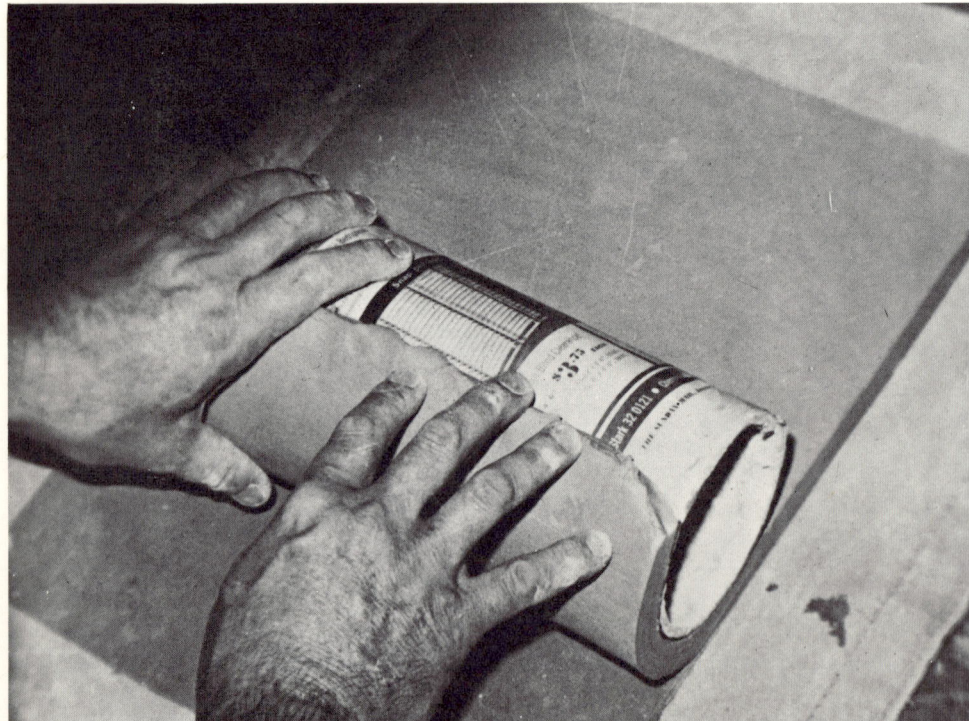

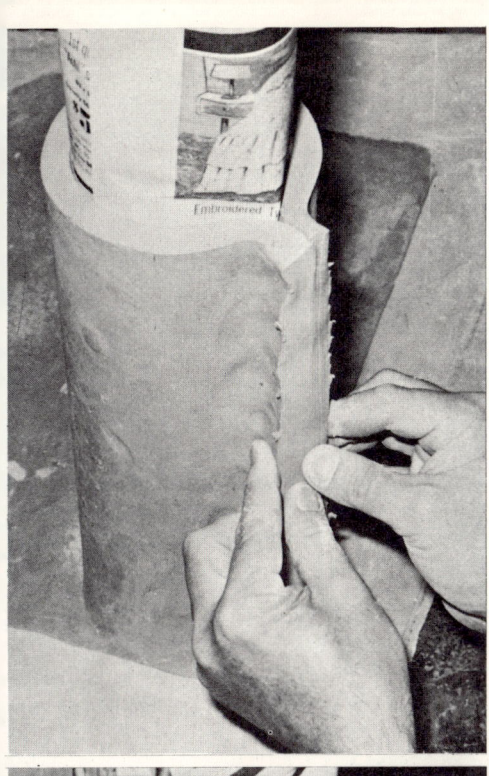

2   Pinch in the sides of the slab and join them.

3   Cut off the excess clay. Smooth the join with a flexible kidney rubber.

4   Place the cylinder on another slab of clay. Cut a circle slightly larger than the base diameter of the cylinder. This circle will form the base. Smear the base with slurry where the cylinder will join it.

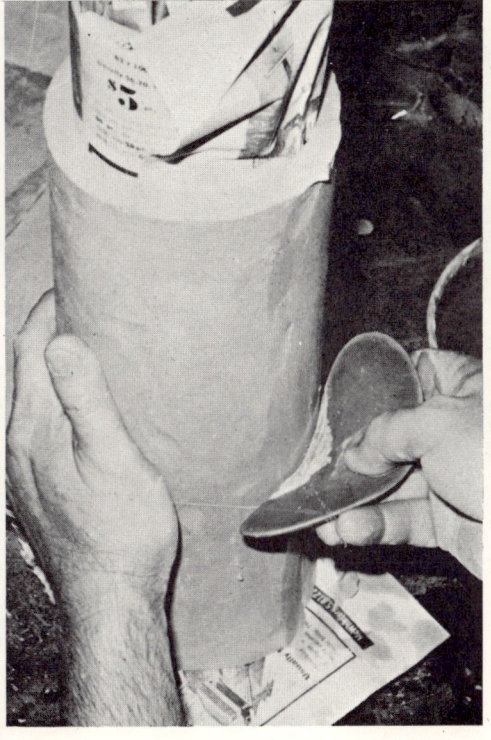
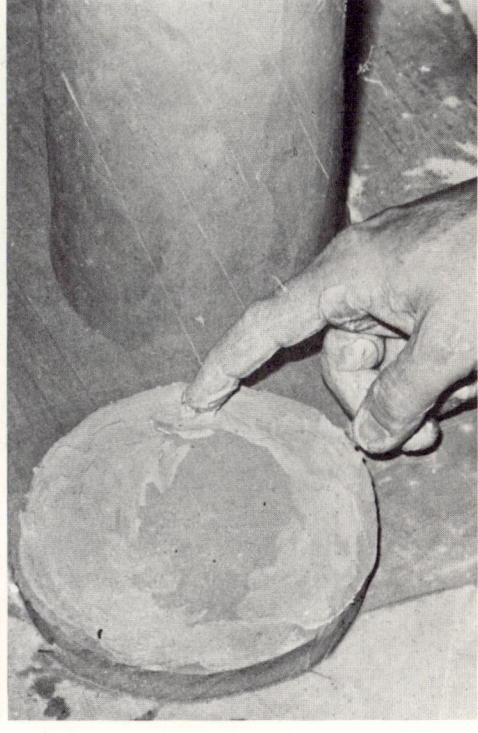

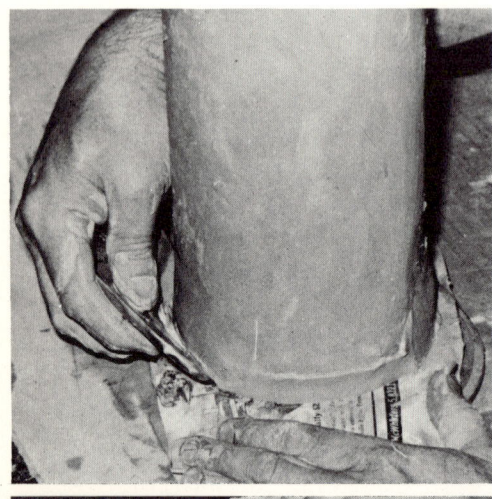

5   Place the cylinder on the base. Draw the excess clay upwards to weld the two pieces together.

6   Grasp the cardboard cylinder and draw it up through the paper. Then remove the paper from inside the clay cylinder.

7   Weld the joins inside the cylinder with thin sausages of clay. Even up the thickness of the clay. From here you can go on and make its shape ready for making into a bottle or lamp base.

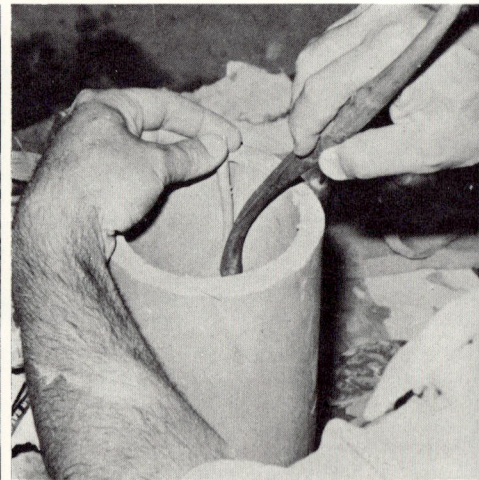

4. design and decoration

Design

Personal taste in design is something that grows. It is a gradually expanding knowledge passing from the obvious local conceptions to an understanding of historical work from primitive times until today. If this learning is done logically, a sound foundation will be built. By now, it should be obvious that the nature of the potter's working material has a great influence on the finished design of the piece. The design fully suggests itself only when the clay is manipulated and the restraints and liberties to be taken with it become evident.

About the time of Christ, pottery in all its forms was being made with a free vigorous strength for household or religious purposes in most parts of the world. In mediaeval times these qualities increased and gave us a virile tradition. Mass production brought about general lowering of standards. Clay was used like wood, metal or stone and aborted into unnatural productions. Designers imitated Asian and Greek pottery without understanding or taste, and our immediate ancestors had their pottery presented to them in many unnatural clay forms. Fortunately, it recently became the policy for industrial designers to work in the medium in which they were to design. As a result of this there has been a sudden raising of standards in work all over the world. Conception of form is influenced by the material and function. Much fine art pottery being made uses simple, balanced proportions and restrained glazes in functional shapes. Another strong trend is in free, sculptural, non-functional forms.

When considering design, return to nature for ideas. Study the stones shaped by water in watercourses and on the seafront. Look at the way melons, gourds and other vegetables and fruits swell from inward growth. If a design is functional, consideration must be given to the demands of the function. Another consideration will be where the object is to be used. The ware's function always affects the type of clay and glaze desirable. When all these factors are considered, a compromise may be necessary to balance function and design. Many ceramic forms may have no precise function at all. They may be purely decorative — wall or garden ornaments, sculptural forms — forms designed to give pleasure to the eye or the touch.

Whether your design is functional or not it must be highly individual. When an approach is forced, because it is 'the thing to do', boring results can be anticipated. Design expression should be natural and unforced, within the capability and understanding of the moment. Small enjoyment will be gained by being somebody else. The problem is to find oneself.

Slip on clay

Slips made with clay and water (which must shrink at about the same rate as the main body) may be applied by dipping, pouring, trailing, brushing, pouring on mesh, applied with a palette knife or any other way which may suggest itself to the imagination of the potter. Slips are usually applied in a thick cream-like mixture. These slips may be coloured with oxides to contrast or harmonise with the body of the pot. Coarse ingredients such as grog and sands may be added. They are usually applied to the pot just as it is made or when it is leather-hard. If they are used on dry or biscuit ware the plastic ingredients are calcined. Wax-resist decoration may be used with skip decoration to create a design.

1 A slip being poured onto a slowly rotating pot. The slip then settles down to form the decoration.

2 The finished pot.

Textures applied to surfaces

Textures may be applied to clay with the use of an open-weave material, such as onion sacking, mosquito netting, dish cloth and any similar material. The material should be slightly dampened so it will cling to the pot.

1 A damp open-weave cloth is wrapped around a bottle. Plastic clay is pressed through the mesh which is then carefully removed and the texture is revealed. If some of the clay pulls off with the mesh, place the mesh back on the pot surface and apply some more clay. Dampen the finger and round any rough or sharp edges. Tap down any loose pieces onto the surface. The coarser the mesh used the higher the decoration will be on the surface.

2 Further decoration can be gained with common household objects applied in an infinite number of ways. Glaze usually pools in the impressions or pulls away from the edges to emphasize the design.

5. colour

General

In the decoration of pottery, primitive people have used the ochres found within clay bodies giving a simple colour range. As knowledge grew, impure metallic oxides were used to give a variety of colours. Most early Chinese pottery was coloured by the use of only iron or copper, with cobalt being introduced later. Modern technology has given a practically unlimited palette to the potter. But its use is of dubious benefit to the artist-potter.

For the very reasons the technologist rejects the use of various materials the artist-potter accepts them. Standardized mass production requires rigidly defined, highly refined and controlled colours. But, in most cases, these colours lack charm and variation of the oxide in its near raw state. Some commercial colours are useful, however, to add subtle variations to oxides. Although many experiments in the use of bright colours are made by the student, his ultimate choice will usually be the oxides which seem to harmonize so well with the nature of clay and stone.

The use of the clay itself as a means of expression must first be considered. The fired surfaces of many clay bodies have sufficient colour, and textural interest to be left unglazed, at least in part, or revealed under a transparent glaze.

Oxides may be added to the clay to vary the body colour. Speckled effects may be gained with manganese and ilmenite. White or coloured grog will add a further character. The potter will find metallic filings, and other minerals may fire to some advantage in the body. The hue and tone of the oxides is affected by the quantity used, the colour of the clay body, the nature of the glaze and the temperature and atmosphere of the kiln.

To have a conception of the palette available, metallic oxides such as iron, copper, cobalt, manganese and chrome may be mixed with water and applied in cross hatched stripes on a clay form, preferably having both vertical and horizontal surfaces. This can then be biscuited, glazed and fired. If these test pieces have a hole in them they can then be hung on the studio wall for visual reference. This can be done with the oxides related to the glaze by being under, in and on it, and glazed by the selected glazes in use in the studio. Of course, only experience will show the proportions in which the colours can be used to best advantage — the proportion of warm to cool, dark to light, liquid to stable and so on.

You can also experiment with the effects gained by firing the clay in different ways. By oxidizing, you can produce one colour from the oxide. By *reducing* (removing oxygen) you can produce another colour from the same oxide. Different glazes will give varying results from the same oxide. Minerals such as zinc, nickel, silica, or zircon will affect the nature of the colour. It is from this knowledge that skill is acquired to express the use of colour in a personal way.

Vehicles or mediums colour for applying

The simplest application of colour is to slip-coat the piece with coloured clay. Slip, or liquid clay, is usually applied to the leather-hard ware, but may be used on bone dry pieces. If the slip has the same shrinkage as the leather-hard ware it will hold well. If it shrinks to a greater extent than the piece, some silica or similar filler should be added. When the slip shrinks less than the leather-hard piece, it may be used on bone dry pieces. Thickness of application is governed by the desired effect and the ability of the slip not to crack if applied very thickly.

The distinction between the terms 'slip' and 'engobe' is small. But engobe is usually taken to mean a compounded slip of finer quality material than that of the piece which it covers. It is often used on dry or biscuit-fired pieces. Compounding an engobe conforms to the same rules as making a slip. Such a compound can consist of a clay, flux, filler, hardener, or opacifier and colouring oxides. Water is usually used as the medium for application. Applying the engobe at the leather-hard stage is, perhaps, the easiest, and gives greater versatility, allowing *graffitto*, that is encising through the engobe coat, to reveal the under surface.

A common engobe composition for this is:
Kaolin: 25 percent Silica: 20 percent
Ball Clay: 25 percent Zirconium: 5 percent
Feldspar: 20 percent Borax: 5 percent

For application on dry surfaces the clay content should be halved. Quantities of oxide for colouring are approximately the same as the list on page 79. Many combinations of these oxides may be made to various shades.

Application may be made in many ways such as dipping, pouring, brushing, spraying, sponging, slip trailing and so on. Wax resist may also be used. The stronger oxides in engobes may bleed through white and opaque glazes, usually in an attractive manner.

Underglazes are laid much the same as watercolours in a direct, fluid manner, and usually under a transparent glaze. There is nothing to prevent their use in or on glazes. Simple underglazes may be made with oxides, water, glycerine or gum. Clay may be added to help prevent the colour running. Commercial underglazes are prepared in great numbers. Reliable manufacturers define the limitations of the colour with kiln temperature and atmosphere, but all should be tested. These underglazes usually consist of an oxide, flux and filler specially compounded, calcined and ground to prevent running. If the colour tends to make a glaze crawl, add some *frit* (see Glossary of Terms) to the colour, or apply it more thinly.

The glaze itself may be coloured with oxides, underglazes or a similar commercial stain known as 'glaze stain'. Incomplete mixing may add interest. Some oxides will cause the glaze to run. If a test indicates that this will happen, some calcined clay should be added.

Colour may be brushed, sprayed or poured on top of a glaze. In pouring a double layer of coloured glaze only minimum time should elapse between applications to prevent lifting through shrinkage.

Glue may be added to prevent damage when handling. A light spray of glaze over the decoration will also do the job. This is of help if the colour is rather refractory and coarse to the touch after firing.

Oxides mixed with a stable glaze such as grass ash, of a different quality to the dipped glaze, will give contrast and depth. Incised patterns may be made through an oxide sprayed over the glazed ware. Glaze deliberately applied roughly, or in runs may be side sprayed, and the rough ridges dusted with a fine dry brush to gain character. Wax resist can also be used. An oxide or coloured glaze may be brushed or sprayed over the base glaze. Matt iron glazes usually brush and sit well on top of another glaze.

These applications can continue endlessly, and forethought should be given to the final aesthetic result. Here the potter is on his own.

A guide to proportions of oxides for colour

The oxides which colour the neutral tones of the base glaze are in addition to the original formula of the glaze. Therefore their percentage is described as 'by addition'. As the proportions of colouring oxides vary considerably to attain the tone and hue desired the convenience of this practice will soon be recognized. In some cases a number of oxides must be used to obtain a colour.

Tests should always be made before making large quantities of coloured glaze. The oxides added may act as a flux on certain glazes, and the addition of clay may be necessary to counter these fluxing effects. In this general guide given below, the colours may be used for either oxidizing or reducing firing unless stated otherwise.

black An overload of cobalt, iron, copper, manganese or ilmenite will give black. A combined 2 to 3 percent of any three of these oxides will be suitable. A combination of cobalt (1 percent); iron (8 percent); manganese (3 percent).

white	Six percent of tin will give a dense white. As tin is expensive, many potters use 8 percent zirconium. The mineral sand companies can supply micro-mesh zirconium, which is most suitable.
yellow	Low toned yellowish hues can be gained by the use of rutile and dolomite in reduction firing only. Six percent vanadium gives yellow when oxidizing firing.
green	Copper, 1 to 5 percent, fires to green in an oxidizing fire. Chrome at 2 percent, and iron at 1 to 3 percent will give green.
blue green	A combination of ½ percent cobalt and 2 percent copper will produce blue-green when oxidizing firing. If reduction is chosen ½ percent cobalt and 1 percent chrome should be used.
blue	When the powerful colourant cobalt is used here ¼ to 1 percent is needed. Small additions of iron, or other oxides will modify the characteristic hardness of this oxide.
red	Rich, low toned reds are made with 5 to 10 percent iron. The transmutation of copper in reduction firing results in red, using ½ to 1 percent.
tan	Tan is gained with 2 percent iron, fired in an oxidizing atmosphere, or 5 percent rutile in either fire.
brown	A warm red brown can be created with 4 to 6 percent iron with an oxidizing firing. A rich speckled brown will result using 3 to 5 percent ilmenite in a reduction fire. 5 percent manganese in either oxidizing or reduction fire will produce another shade of brown.

6. glazing

General

A glaze can be a moment of frozen beauty . . . a liquid held in suspension for time infinite. Stoneware glazes have a unique character not obtainable in the glazes of other types of pottery. By the very use of partly refined materials, results of unique quality occur. At times, by some freak of the fire, they can be breathtaking

The function of the glaze dictates its type and manner of use. If the piece is solely decorative, anything goes. If function is a factor, consideration should be given to this restraint.

Commercial pottery has adopted the expediency of uniformity. The materials used in its creation are refined and selected for a positive result — conformity to a standard. Creative pottery has no such restraint and may be as fine or as coarse as desired. So with the glaze. Effects which would send a commercial potter screaming because they upset his preconceived ideas may be of interest to the artist-potter.

Most beginners, as beginners always will be, are interested in the most bizarre and complex combinations of glaze. As wisdom grows with experience, the beauty of limited means becomes apparent. Simplicity of form and glaze gives a strength and beauty not found in most overstated and overglazed shapes.

The glaze is made of various minerals suspended in water. When a glaze is typed, it is usually typed by its chief fluxing agent. Commonplace local materials may be used, and refinement often only robs the glaze of character.

The ware is 'raw' in its clay state, or 'biscuited', by a low preliminary fire. Biscuited ware is easier to handle when glazing and loading into the kiln. Once fired pottery usually has a better fitting glaze and a different character. It is more suitable for slip decoration and work with surface qualities which the potter wants to emphasize.

Methods of applying glazes

Dipping is the most used method of glazing. The article is first cleaned and then plunged into the liquid glaze. It is removed in such a way that it has a fairly even covering of glaze. If a piece is large, either the glaze should be thinned with extra water until it lightly covers the hand when dipped in, or the ware should be wetted so that it will only accept a certain amount of glaze. If two or more glazes are superimposed, obviously the first glaze or glazes should be thinner. Also in this case, it may be necessary to add glue or clay to help bind the glaze to the piece and prevent crawling.

If the ware is being once fired it is imperative that dip glazing be done at exactly the right time in order not to crack the piece. This state on most clays is slightly drier than leather-hard. But it can be even drier according to the body used. The glaze must have sufficient clay in it to shrink with the clay body, which will have slightly expanded during the dipping procedure. About thirty-five percent clay or ten percent bentonite is a rough proportion.

Slip glazing may be used. In this case, a clay which melts at a lower temperature than the maturing temperature of the kiln, or a clay with fluxes added to it so it will do this, can be used. If this glaze cracks and peels off the ware, the clay for it can be *calcined* — that is fired to about red heat and then ground if necessary. This method will solve this problem.

For dipping you often need enough glaze in which to dip a fairly large article. As this is not always possible, you may have to make use of other methods of glazing.

Brushing is one such way. This should be done quickly on a slightly wetted surface to prevent too great a build up of glaze. It is an excellent method of glaze decoration.

Pouring is faster and more versatile. Once again, if the biscuit ware is dampened, greater control may be attained to prevent 'build-up' of glaze. Fast, sure action is essential to gain an even coat. With many glazes, an uneven surface can be very attractive, showing the run lines on the surface in whatever direction the glazer decides. A spray of oxides from one side to shadow and emphasize may further enhance the glaze. Pouring gives many opportunities for decoration over another glaze. When pouring a glaze, watch the 'build-up' on the edges.

Dampen the edges well and they will repel some of the glaze and so remain fairly even. If they are slightly thin, it is a simple matter to brush a little more on once the glaze has dried. A flexible wrist, a brave pouring hand and a slightly damp surface are the best ingredients for the success of poured glazes. Sprayed glazes are most suitable for once fired pottery because the wetting qualities are reduced to a minimum and the thickness of glaze may be layered at will.

Many ingredients of stoneware glazes are harmless. But copper carbonate, barium carbonate, manganese and others are not. Dusts in a pottery are positively harmful to the lungs. It is essential that a fan should be used with indoor spraying to exhaust these fumes from the building, or a mask should be worn.

In all cases, the thickness required can only be known from practice, because the glaze may be so thin as to merely seal the clay, or so thick to be as unctuous as the impasto of an oil painting. Some glazes will run exceedingly or craze if too thick. Others are dry and uninteresting if too thin. When double dipping is used, only knowledge of the glazes will prevent the catastrophe of putting a runny glaze on an easily fluxed base glaze. Glazes which are indifferent on their own sometimes work well one over the other. Stable glazes are the godsend to the potter, but fluid glazes will often be the ones which give the heavenly results.

Preparing different types of glazes

The materials required to make glaze will be containers, sieves of about sixty and one hundred mesh, fly screen, rubber gloves, dippers, scales, water and the glaze ingredients, and a felt ink pencil to label the container. The scales should have a sizable tray to hold the ingredients. Estimate the required quantity of dry ingredients to make sufficient glaze to fill the container. About five pounds of dry materials are used to a gallon of water. The solids are always added to the liquid, and 'difficult' ingredients such as talc, ash and clays which need wetting are weighed out and added first, or mixed well with the other ingredients dry. These should not be disturbed as they are wetting, but insoluble materials such as silica and feldspar can be placed on top of them to push them under the water. If need be, add an excess of water to allow easy initial sieving. This excess is easily decanted later. Sieve several times if a harmonious blend is desired.

One of the advantages of high fired pottery is that the glazes can be made of simple local materials. There are many common substances which will melt to a glass at temperatures of 1200 to 1300 degrees Centigrade.

The simplest of all glazes are slip glazes which have been described. Many common red clays are suitable for such a glaze. If it is to be applied to the raw ware, it should shrink at a similar rate to the leather-hard pot. If it should crack off, then it may be necessary to calcine the clay over 600 deg. C. It may need to be ground after this process but it will then act as any dry inert glaze and can be used on biscuit ware. If the clay does not melt to a glaze at the temperature fired to, a flux can be added. The manner of application and firing gives the variation of results. These glazes are usually in the brown and red-orange colours. But oxides may be added to vary the colour. A good slip glaze will also increase the mechanical strength of the body from fifty to a hundred percent.

Salt glazes evidently originated in Germany. This type of glazing is simple and quietly attractive. Colours can be applied to the ware as underglaze and these will show through the glaze. With the addition of about equal parts of borax, this type of glazing can be done as low as 900 deg. C. with some success. But, a temperature of over 1200 deg. C. is desirable for best results. In stoneware firing, the salt, often in the form of wet coarse rock salt, is added near the burners at about 1250 deg. C. in a reducing atmosphere. It may be necessary to *bait* (throw in salt) three or four times. As each lot of salt is thrown into the fire, the temperature will fall. This should be allowed to rise again before further baiting. The use of up to fifteen percent borax or boric acid, particularly in the last baiting will improve the glaze. The salt is vaporized and will cover everything in the kiln. The shelves should be painted with kiln-wash. As the kiln has continued salt firings, the residue on the walls will vaporize in firing with the result that less salt has to be added. The fumes from the kiln are dangerous and should be exhausted from the building if the kiln is inside.

Test rings may be placed near the spy hole from where they can be hooked out and examined to check the glaze thickness. The vapour from this glaze may not find its way into shapes like bottles and vases, and these may need to be glazed in these parts before firing.

Once a kiln is used for a salt glazing, the inside of it is coated with glaze. In an electric kiln this is disastrous. If it is desired to fire some salt glazed pieces without ruining the kiln for other work, this can be done by firing the pieces in a sealed *saggar* (a refractory box) which has its inside coated with salt and borax. The vapour caused by these ingredients volatilizing will coat the ware thinly.

Consideration will now be given to stoneware glazes which are applied as definite coatings on the ware, and fired between 1250 and 1300 deg. C. A reducing atmosphere induced between about 1100 and 1250 deg. C. with at least half an hour oxidation at the end of the fire is usually an excellent manner of firing these glazes.

One of the most interesting fields of glaze is that of ash glazing. Ash from vegetation contains all of the ingredients for glaze, but of course not in a balanced manner. These ingredients include potash and soda. Potters with tender skins should wear gloves. This ash also contains amounts of alumina, iron, calcium, magnesia, sodium, silica, phosphorus and other minerals.

In most cases, the larger the tree, the softer and more fluid the glaze. The hard stable glazes come from the grasses, including bamboo, rice, and wheat, they also come from fast growing weeds and shrubs, all of which are high in silica content. Ash glazes on their own cover a wide range and are usually easy to handle. They are most suitable for double dipping and look well with a wax resist design. They lend themselves to further decoration, if desired, by the use of oxides mixed with them or sprayed or brushed on them. If the ash runs excessively, add calcined kaolin, by experiment, until the glaze behaves as desired.

Ash glazes may be made with clay and feldspar. One such glaze fired at 1250-1280 deg. C. is as follows:

Ash: 35 percent
Feldspar: 35 percent
Ball Clay: 15 percent
Talc: 15 percent

If a running, overfluxed glaze is made, it can be used with discretion to make a fluid decoration on ware. Stable ash glaze with oxides added is useful for rigid formal design. When a glaze is dry, some ash added to it can bring it to life. With a kiln test the nature of the ash in the glaze can be quickly observed and adjusted for the requirements desired.

In Asia, ash, feldspar, iron and common red clay were used to produce many glazes. Ash, feldspar and iron made many celadon glazes. Ash, lime, feldspar and common red clays were the base of the many variations of iron glazes used. These glazes remain practically unaltered today in Asia.

Iron matt glazes are most useful. They make a fine base for double dipping and also work well as a top glaze on a light base. For brushwork and edging other glazes, they are reliable in every way. One of these glazes most used in our pottery is fired at 1250 to 1280 deg. C. If applied thinly over another glaze, a green hue is usually obtained. Its composition is as follows:

Potash Feldspar: 60 percent
Calcined Kaolin: 18 percent
Silica: 5 percent
Whiting: 2 percent
Talc: 15 percent
Iron: 10 percent by addition

If it should be needed, three percent bentonite (with an equivalent reduction of kaolin) or some synthetic resin glue will assist to bind these glazes tightly to the pot.

Celadon glaze which gives colour from grey blues to green, gloss or matt, was mainly iron and wood ash as originally used in Asia. Many potters today use a feldspathic glaze as a base to make a celadon glaze and gain variety by adding iron.
1-3 percent gives brown to treacly black
10-15 percent gives metallic purple.
Generally the glaze is applied quite heavily. It is fired under reducing conditions subsequently oxidizing well at the completion of the firing to improve the glaze surface. Larger quantities of iron with perhaps some wood ash added, the glaze being heavily applied and fired under smoky reducing atmosphere, will give *temmoku* effects, browns and khakis changed to blacks and blues.

Many glazes can be made by adding iron, ochres, or the rutile-ilmenite family to various base glazes in different quantities and firing in reducing conditions of varying degree. Crudely prepared materials fired slowly under smoky conditions yield the most original results. Care must be taken when using iron as it tends to act as a flux and cause the glaze to run.

Feldspar is the most common flux used by the potter in stoneware firing. In Asia, simple feldspathic glazes were generally used when high firing was introduced. Some, it is said, were made only from feldspathic stone, or even parts of such natural feldspar and woodash. The use of local impure feldspars gave character to the ware of these potters and indicated the area of origin of the work.

One source of silica was ash of plants rich in this mineral, such as rice straw and fern-leaf. One such glaze fired at 1250 to 1280 deg. C. consisted of:

Feldspar: 20 percent
Rice Straw Ash: 80 percent

Copper-red was achieved by using a copper slip under the glaze or adding copper to the glaze. Iron and other oxide-bearing minerals were used to vary the glaze.

The Western practice has been to use more refined materials in calculating glaze composition. There are hundreds of useful glazes. Study of other books on glazing will give many proven examples.

A fairly stable feldspathic glaze, clear at 1280 deg. C. but milky if underfired, is as follows:

Feldspar: 44 percent   Kaolin: 10 percent
Whiting: 18 percent   Silica: 28 percent

Limestone glazes are simple and beautiful. Usually they are composed from the maximum quantity of limestone able to be used. Whiting, a calcium carbonate, is used to supply lime. Firing temperature is 1260 to 1280 deg. C. for these two examples.

Example 1
Silica: 30 percent
Whiting: 25 percent
Feldspar: 35 percent
Clay: 10 percent

Example 2
Feldspar: 80 percent
Whiting: 20 percent

Dolomite or talc are two minerals usually chosen to provide the magnesia which makes the distinctive smoothness of magnesia glazes.

Example 1
Feldspar: 25 percent
Whiting: 11 percent
Talc: 15 percent
China clay: 14 percent
Silica: 25 percent

Example 2
Feldspar: 40 percent
Clay: 15 percent
Talc: 15 percent
Ash: 30 percent

Fire between 1250 and 1280 deg. C. Use oxidizing or reducing fire.

Matt glazes result when the glaze crystallizes. The term is used rather loosely in pottery, generally referring to a glaze with the minimum of reflective qualities. The simplest matt glaze is obtained by increasing the alumina (supplied by clay). Other matt effects can be produced by increasing the ratio of more refractory fluxes such as barium, lime and magnesia. Overloading the glaze with iron, manganese, zinc or rutile will give interesting matt crystalline surfaces.

The cooling cycle must be controlled. Slower cooling at the stiffening to freezing point of the glaze encourages these effects. Too fast cooling may give a bright glaze. Some kilns have a naturally slow cooling rate and crystallization is quite simple to achieve. Others will require some control through continued firing, but on a diminishing scale after the glaze maturity temperature has been reached.

While matt glazes are beautiful, some have a surface which may be unsuitable for some functions. Some give forth scratching sounds when eaten from with knife and fork and may be hard to clean. Two suggestions to be fired at 1250 to 1300 deg. C. preferably by reducing fire, are as follows:

Example 1
Talc: 30 percent
Whiting: 25 percent
Feldspar: 34 percent
Silica: 11 percent
Rutile: 2 percent by addition

Example 2
Feldspar: 45 percent
Clay: 25 percent
Dolomite: 25 percent
Whiting: 5 percent

The addition of twenty percent each of whiting and china clay to sixty percent glaze will perhaps produce a quiet matt surface. Tests will show which glazes work well and which become dull and uninteresting.

Opaque glazes are made by the addition of a substance to reflect light. The common minerals used are tin oxide and zircon, either alone or together. About five percent of tin oxide or ten percent of micromesh zircon may be used.

Local rocks are a further interesting source of glazes. The material to make these may be obtained either in the field or by gathering it in the form of fine dust under machinery being used at quarries or masonry works for crushing or cutting stone.

While gaining experience, use the softer rocks which are easy to crush. The fine dust may be mixed with perhaps ten to fifteen percent bentonite which not only adds alumina to the glaze but acts as a binder. Wood ash may also be added to the glaze.

Suggestions to fire at 1280 to 1300 deg. C. are as follows:

Example 1
Clay: 15 percent
Rock: 85 percent

Example 2
Clay: 15 percent
Rock: 45 percent
Ash: 40 percent

Example 3
Clay: 15 percent
Rock: 25 percent
Ash: 60 percent

Take precautions against the glaze running when tests are being made.

Glaze faults

Glazes are composed of materials having varying expansion and contraction rates. The clay body also undergoes complex contraction while cooling. The potter aims to balance these factors to obtain 'glaze fit'.

Crazing is the cracking of the glaze on the finished article. There are two sorts of crazing — 'immediate' and 'delayed'. Ideally, the body should contract very slightly more than the glaze, thus holding the glaze in a state of compression. If this is not the case, the glaze, being under tension, may craze immediately on being taken from the kiln. This crazing occurs because the glaze contracts more than it should.

Shivering is the opposite effect to crazing. In this case, the body has greater expansion than the glaze, contracting more and causing the body to shrink to a greater extent than the glaze can contract to. As a result, the glaze peels off or shivers. Shivering is generally attributed to excessive silica in the body. If silica has been added to the body, reduce the quantity. If the clay is naturally excessive in silica, add a less siliceous clay, add high-alumina grog, or use more feldspar.

The potter tries to tread the middle path. If crazing occurs, add silica to both or either the body and glaze, usually the glaze, in small additions. If any shivering results, then reduce the body silica slightly. A guide to follow is:
Not enough silica in glaze or body — crazing
Proper proportions — sound glaze
Too great a quantity of silica — shivering.

Crawling is a condition where the glaze pulls back to reveal the body surface. This can be caused by glazing dusty or oily ware. Where an underglaze is applied too heavily, it may prevent the glaze adhering to the body. The glaze will then draw back off this surface during firing.

When a glaze is double dipped, or if the adherence of a base glaze on the ware is lessened through some cause, such as excessive shrinkage resulting from too much plastic clay in the glaze, it will crack and contract during the tensions of firing. This can be prevented by either cleaning the ware thoroughly, by adding calcined clay in the glaze or by adding a binder to assist adhesion.

Pouring a heavy glaze over a dry base glaze will break the adherence of the base glaze to the piece and cause crawling. When double dipping, apply the second glaze quickly before the base glaze is dry or add a binder to the base glaze.

Running is caused either by a glaze being fired too high or applied too heavily. Either way, the glaze may run down to stick the ware to the kiln shelf. Altering the ratio between the fluxing and refractory parts of the glaze will rectify the first point. Heavy application is caused not only from having the glaze too thick, but not stirring it thoroughly, so that when the piece is dipped, one part is glazed too thinly and the other part has a heavy layer of glaze on it. Some glazes will act as fluxes to each other, so watch this when double dipping. Load the kiln where possible so that the variance of temperature in the kiln is in harmony with the type of glaze placed in each part.

Dry Glazes can be rectified quickly by the addition of a quantity of suitable flux. Where the glaze has a rough surface from the use of refractory colours on it, a thin coating of glaze sprayed or brushed over the piece will make it more pleasant to the touch. If ware that is still damp from glazing is placed in the kiln and heat is rapidly applied, crawling or blistering may result.

Further faults, not connected with the glaze, may be caused by small pieces of refractory material dropping from the kiln roof or from under the kiln shelves. Brush these kiln surfaces well. If this does happen, often the offending material can be chipped or ground off, the flaw reglazed and the piece refired.

Never fire untested clay or glaze. When glass is used in the ware, to make a heavy glass mass inside the piece, be sure the ware has a strong base. Otherwise the base may crack and the glaze run through. Many faults and uninteresting glazes can be cured with a second firing. Sympathy with the glazes and materials being used and intelligent pottery procedure will prevent most faults.

Glazing a bottle

1 Some glaze is poured into the bottle. The bottle is then rotated as the glaze is poured out so that all the interior is coated.

2 As this piece is too large for the bucket, one end is dipped ...

3 ... And then the other, and the glaze is removed from the foot.

4 Another glaze being poured onto the bottle after a wax design has been applied to one side.

7. kilns

Types of Kilns

From primitive times, when humans first learned to harden clay by fire, many more kiln designs have been conceived than there is space in this book to describe. Even today, African women heap their handbuilt water and cooking bowls one on the other and fire them in the open with dry grass or maize to give a low-fired cheap and thermal shock resistant pottery of traditional beauty. Trench kilns and open walled kilns are also still in use, giving the further refinement of containing the heat to some degree.

Bank kilns may have been the next innovation. A chamber was built in the side of a hill through which the heat had to pass. This enclosed combustion chamber, with its primitive firebox and flues, gave the potter a kiln to reach higher temperatures. These kilns were up-draught kilns where the hot gases passed directly through the kiln. Much heat was wasted even though maximum use was made of skilful stoking and stacking. In Asia today, this type of kiln is still in use but in a refined version.

Most modern potters use down-draught kilns fired with wood, gas, coke, coal or oil. This gives maximum efficiency for a small intermittent kiln. There are many alternate designs, some of which will be described.

Electricity gives radiant heat, and many electrical kilns are built to give clean conditions of firing in any surroundings.

The best way to learn about kilns is to build a Raku kiln, and fire it. The construction is of loose bricks and the kiln may be easily rebuilt in many designs. It costs very little to build and fire. Other kilns discussed here will cost quite a lot, particularly when expensive refractory insulating bricks are used.

Fuel is a major influence in deciding the type of kiln to build. Wood kilns are impossible in a closely built area. In recent years, liquid petroleum gas has become readily available. This fuel is useful where town or natural gas is not available. In a built-up area, the choice lies between electricity, gas, or liquid petroleum gas. In open areas, wood, electricity, liquid gas or oil can be used. The use of coke depends on the supply of a high class material.

Kiln construction can be of loose bricks as a Raku kiln is built, the fairly loose construction of a catenary arch kiln, or mortared brickwork, sometimes contained in a metal box. It is apparent with experience of building small kilns, the advantages gained by using refractory insulating bricks which are precise in shape, easy to handle and shape, and give greater efficiency, although they are more expensive than the common firebricks and often do not last as long.

Probably no kiln can be designed which has every quality. Different potters have various conceptions of the work they wish to do and the kiln must fit these demands. But, make sure the kiln, or the materials it is to be built of, fulfil its requirements by specifying its work such as 'firing to 1300 degrees Centigrade under oxidizing and reducing conditions, ten hours firing, fifty hours cooling and gas burning'. The material suppliers then have definite qualities to meet. For instance, some ceramic cements will not stand reduction firing and some bricks will not withstand direct flame impingement.

It is a further mistake to go to the opposite extreme and use materials of a quality made for much greater heat than that to be used. The suppliers will explain these are not ideal for many reasons. Much research and care has been taken to make specific qualities for the various temperatures.

Like any machine, it is important that replacement parts are readily available and easily installed.

Considerable expansion will take place with high temperatures and allowance must be made for it.

If there is an area where one can be liberal it is with the supply of heat. A wood kiln with a firebox that is too small, a gas or oil kiln with small diameter pipes and an electric kiln with insufficient power input will all take a long time to reach the required temperature. As long as delicate control can be kept, reserves of heat are desirable.

Provided the ware is not subjected to *hot spots* (greater heat in one spot), the type of firing being discussed in this book, can be fired openly without a *muffle* (protective space) or *saggars* (protective boxes).

Earthenware oxidized glazes using lead require a clean atmosphere. High temperature stoneware glazes are less fastidious, because lead is practically never used.

Insulation should be of a type which will minimize the loss of heat by insuring the prevention of the major means of heat dissipation, conduction and radiation — heat losses through the material, or convection losses through air spaces.

Insulation is basically achieved by using the poor conductivity of air. Heat passes through solids by conduction, and through open spaces by radiation and convection. Loose diatomaceous earth ideally fulfils these requirements because of its fine, but porous grains. In one case, where a kiln was built on a slope, a load of ashes poured over it, except for the loading door and fire box, proved efficient insulation. Solid insulating concrete mixes and insulating brick are very good. But cracks usually appear which invite convection losses.

A recent product, insulating alumina-silica blanket sold as Kaowool, can be draped over the kiln's external surface to give excellent insulating qualities.

A catenary arch liquid petroleum gas fired kiln.

Preparations for firing

1   A biscuit kiln stacked ready for firing.
2   A kiln showing pieces after glaze firing. Observe the cones.

Main fuels

Gas is easily controlled, and requires no hard work. The kiln can be left for known periods once its rate of climb is established. The flame is clean and firings can be done in confined spaces provided there is adequate ventilation and exhaust. Gas, in one of its types, is well worth considering even though it may not be the cheapest fuel.

Electricity gives heat by radiation and the results are visibly different from heat by combustion. An electric kiln can be burnt in the same conditions as a large kitchen stove, because the heat is contained in a well insulated box, and the controls are easy to manage and efficient. Electricity is the most convenient of the fuels, but the firing results are limited. The advantages of the convenience will outweigh the defects to some potters when choosing a kiln. Do not wire an electrical kiln without technical assistance. It is dangerous and probably an offence under local law.

Wood and Charcoal Immense satisfaction can be derived from the use of wood firing. The whole procedure is an artistic drama. Through knowledge one gains a sympathy with the fire and an ability to detect reasons for insufficient rise of temperature or poor firing conditions. It is also hard, tiring work to fire a wood kiln for twelve or more hours. One has to judge whether the sore eyes, tired muscles and soot and dirt are worth the results. Many potters think they are. There is no better way of finding out than to fire a Raku kiln and no lesson could be any cheaper.

    For a stoneware firing a large quantity of wood will be needed. During reduction there will be large amounts of smoke and soot. It is advisable to have space and accommodating neighbours. You can obtain fuel from a wood cutter, timber mill or a furniture maker who will have offcuts. The fuel must have a high calorific value.

Ordinary firebricks rather than insulating firebricks are the best to use because there is considerable abrasion in this type of kiln, particularly in the general idea of the firebox and bagwall. Every potter should try wood firing to learn lessons about the kiln that more sophisticated methods of firing will not teach.

Oil is used under air pressure with special burners or with simple drip feed burners by art-potters. Both forms of firing can yield smoke and soot if neglected. It was once thought that oil firing using pressure burners caused rapid deterioration of kiln walls. Later investigation has shown faulty firing was the main cause of this. Care must be taken to ensure an automatic cut off of oil if the air pressure ceases, because the burning oil, if unchecked, will stream on to the ground.

Many drip-feed kilns have been made and used. It is well to note that these should only be built in a large open area because copious smoke pours out from these kilns even, at times, after firing technique is achieved. The principal is to gravity feed oil to a burner which has natural draught or a simple forced draught system.

This simple means of firing has many variations. Many other designs will work with the burners designed to have the oil dripping on a set of louvres in the fire mouth or specially made burners with air injecting to mix with and atomize the oil.

Many designs have appeared in 'The New Zealand Potter', which can be obtained from Box 12-162, Wellington North, New Zealand. The Japanese have several simple and cheap units for oil burning on the market with burner and blower set-up in one unit.

Whichever kiln is decided upon, become knowledgeable about its character and work within these limitations. With one or two clays, several glazes and oxides and a good kiln the variations of results are infinite.

A Simple Gas Kiln

1   In the first stages of construction two layers of bricks are laid to form the base and part of the walls are constructed. The burner nozzle is level with the floor of the fire box and an area of sixteen square inches is left around the burner nozzle. Three inches have been left under the combustion chamber floor which still has to be placed.

At the next stage of construction just over two inches of space are left between the kiln floor and the back wall for combustion. Allowance is made for the pyrometric thermocouple to be inserted through the wall and more bricks are laid.

2   In the finished kiln. The roof is supported by a tile. But these soft bricks could easily be drilled and supported by a rod, or put in as an arch. The pyrometer is inserted. The three protruding bricks form the door. The chimney flue is level with the top of the kiln, over the burner, its outlet is level with the floor. It is about sixteen square inches also. If unburnt gases can be smelt it must be enlarged.

Downdraught Kiln fired with town gas

Town or natural gas in firing is perhaps the cleanest, most efficient and convenient of all methods to use. Construction is simple and the kiln can be fired to 1300 deg. C. easily without the use of forced draught.

If the kiln is constructed between eight and twenty cubic feet the principles of building do not vary to a great degree.

In the design to be described below the only variations will be in the gas flow and chimney height. The larger the kiln the more gas that will be needed, therefore one or more extra burners will be necessary. A small kiln will have its chimney flue almost level with the crown of the kiln. A kiln with a higher firing chamber will need a correspondingly higher chimney.

Firing kilns of these sizes can be done in six to twelve hours depending on the capacity of the firing chamber and the load in the kiln.

According to cubic capacity four or five burners will be sufficient. These are alternatively placed — two on each side of the kiln.

Various types of burners may be used and an efficient type is a one inch low pressure gas inspirator at four inch water gauge. The kiln will have to be built inside a steel box if loose insulation powder is to be used. Further developments in insulation technique have resulted in the manufacture of an alumina-silica thermal blanket known as Kaowool, which is being used successfully in place of powdered insulation. A steel angle iron frame would still be necessary to brace the arch of the kiln to prevent its collapse during the expansion and contraction of the kiln firing.

High quality insulating refractory brick is economical and easy to use. Although this brick has a high initial cost, its insulating qualities soon save on fuel consumption.

Denser bricks should be used where direct flame impingement occurs at the base of the kiln walls opposite the burners.

When powdered insulation is used (such as diatomaceous earth) an inward pressure will be exerted on the walls. Provision for this pressure should be made during construction by building the walls with a slight outward arch.

Smaller kiln walls should be built using the three inch side of the brick while larger kilns use the four-and-a-half-inch side of the brick.

Insulation is provided by nine inches of powdered insulation, or a recommended thickness of Kaowool blanket. The arch is constructed of insulating refractory bricks or cast in sections using castable refractory, three inches thick. Insulation is done to the same degree.

The doors are made with loose insulating refractory bricks using the three inch side. Any cracks are sealed with a slurry made with sand and a little clay to bind it. Further insulation is provided by another three inches of insulating brick.

One or more spyholes are provided in the door, these should be at least two inches in diameter to allow a good view of the pyrometric cones in the kiln.

Six inches of brickwork is needed under the fireboxes. The flame is channelled under the hearth through four-and-a-half-inch by four-and-a-half-inch flues. These flueways are divided from each other by one inch splits (thin firebricks) four-and-a-half-inches high. The walls so formed also support the kiln floor. The thickness of the floor is decided by experiment. Old cracked kiln shelves can often be used because they are well supported by these walls. A minimum space of two inches is left between the floor and the walls. This gives a space four-and-a-half-inches by two inches opposite each burner for the flame to enter the firing chamber.

Thought must be given to easy maintenance of this part of the kiln, as it is subject to the greatest wear. It should be built so that each part may be independently replaced.

Bag walls (protective walls) are placed parallel to the sides of the kiln wall which directs the fire upwards to the arch. These walls can be made from old kiln shelves. They should not be fixed as this makes for difficult maintenance.

The outlet flues are at floor level. An even heat is gained if two, three inch square outlet flues are placed on each side of the kiln near the door, and a six inch by four-and-a-half-inch flue at the centre back. There are other ways of arranging these flue holes but their area must not be less than stipulated. Larger combustion spaces are required with natural or L.P. gas.

A hole for the pyrometer thermocouple may be provided in the back wall. Dampers are installed at the chimneys to control reduction firing.

Wood firing

Wood firing kilns are the pampered darlings of all kilns. They demand constant attention. The fuel must be cut to the right size and fed at the right time. There is also a considerable art in knowing which is the right size and what is the right time.

To become initiated into the mysteries and skills of wood firing, begin with a small kiln no larger than the one described in this chapter, or better still the Raku kiln, which is so cheaply built and fired. With a large kiln and no skill, the potter may give up in despair of ever being able to reach the required temperature. A change of approach to the method of firing, the way the ware is stacked, the way the shelves are arranged, the use of the damper, the size of the fuel, and so on will assure the right temperature is reached.

Wood in many parts of the world is still plentiful and cheap, and often potteries are sited with convenience to fuel rather than to clay. The local wood supplier will be well aware of the wood with the greatest calorific value. Old-time bakers and users of wood ovens will be able to tell of the best burning and heat-giving woods. Any forestry department will be of help there. The art of wood firing has a different atmosphere to any other. It is a more leisurely process and a much greater intimacy exists between the potter and his flame than in any other type of firing.

The potter will be watching the weather. The rise or fall of atmospheric pressure will have an effect on the firing. The kiln has a constantly changing personality, from the lazy quiet beginning to the dramatic climax of full fire, flame issuing from all ports, and greedy demands for fuel.

Following is a description of a typical firing of a simple twelve cubic foot downdraught wood kiln. The evening before the firing, light a small fire of chips at the front of the fire box. The door of the kiln has the top two courses of brick still off and the chimney flue is wide open. Keep the fire burning gently until bedtime. Rise early the next morning and commence the firing. If the ware is to be once fired, the firing must be slow and the top of the kiln door should be left open until colour appears in the kiln. If the ware has been previously biscuited before glazing, the evening in a warm kiln should have evaporated any moisture and the heat can rise as rapidly as required.

Commence firing with chips and several pieces of wood about one-and-a-half inches in diameter. After 100 deg. C., fuel can be increased. When a glow eventually appears in the kiln, the doorway should be sealed. If the current of cold air passing through the kiln appears too strong, and is preventing the temperature from rising, then reduce the area of flue by partially closing the chimney damper. Watch the pyrometer to see if the adjustment caused a rise of temperature. Efficiency of the position of the damper can be checked by opening the top spy hole in the door then slowly closing the damper until heat is felt to exude from the hole. Slowly open the damper again until no heat is felt, and leave it at this point.

With once fired ware, red heat should be reached, so that all the chemical water is expelled from the ware before rapid increase in firing. The air passing through the firebox is blocked. All air now passes under and up to it through the ash pit.

From now, charge the firebox with wood about three inches in diameter. If the rate of stoking increases with no resultant rise in temperature, close the damper slightly. Observe that sufficient air space is left around the fuel so that ignition is at its maximum at all times. The basic rhythm is continued until about 1150 deg. C. is reached. At this time, the temperature will tend to flatten out. Do not choke the firebox with too much fuel to counter this. Reduce the size of the fuel so that combustion will be faster and feed more often. Warm the timber by stacking it around the fire box. Ash is grey and is dull with air blowing on it. It should be raked out of the firebox as it is performing no useful function. Wood still being burnt may be thought to be ash. But if there is any colour in it, it is in effect charcoal. It should not be disturbed, because it is still effectively creating heat. If this glowing ash falls into the ash pit, rake it to the front of the ash pit to form a mound of glowing coals to preheat the air passing over it as it enters the kiln.

Throughout the firing, rhythm is the basic technique. As fuel is thrown into the firebox a pattern of visible events will be evident. The addition of fuel will create the condition which results in reduction, shown by flame rising from the chimney. As the flame dies, oxidization is in process, and in a short time the fuel has been used and more is required. So a recurring pattern is apparent. Once the rhythmic timing is sensed, the adding of fuel becomes an easily defined system.

While the pyrometer shows a definite rise, and as long as the temperature is rising, do not overstoke. The flue under the fire grate and the chimney flue should be wide open. When the kiln temperature seems slower to rise, reduce the diameter of the wood to half an inch or an inch thickness. Fire like this until 1280 or 1300 deg. C. is reached, or until the *cone* (a device for measuring the work done by the heat) appears ready to drop. A time of mellowing oxidizing conditions is now needed for perhaps half an hour. Open the damper and make sure no flame is showing at the spyhole or chimney. Stoke at a rate which keeps this clear condition.

Upon completion of firing, the firebox and chimney and other openings are entirely blocked after allowing about half an hour for any waste gases to escape.

The kiln has risen to 850 deg. C. during the first ten hours at about 80 deg. C. an hour. Once reduction becomes heavy, this rise drops to about 50 deg. C. an hour. This makes a firing cycle of about seventeen hours to reach 1280 to 1300 deg. C. This cycle may be slower if desired. At least one whole day must pass before the door is slowly opened to unload. The usual cooling period is four times the firing cycle. All apertures are opened slowly when the kiln has cooled.

Raku kilns

Traditional Raku pottery is very low fired earthenware. It is fired in a small kiln. Usually it is associated with making cups for the tea ceremony in Japan.

No more rewarding introduction to pottery can be found for the beginner. Every aspect of pottery is dealt with — preparing the clay, making the pottery, building the kiln and learning how to fire it, mixing glazes and learning how to use them. All this can be achieved in a few days. Of course, you may not necessarily be successful at the beginning.

The clay is usually a fire or stoneware clay, with at least twenty-five percent grog, or as much as can be added without spoiling the workability of the clay. Any method of making may be used. After the ware is made and dried, it is biscuit fired at about 800-900 deg. C.

Making the kiln is a simple matter and takes only about an hour the first time and once the principles are mastered it is a simple adaptation to vary the size of the firing chamber. About 150 full and thirty half bricks, (preferably fire bricks, but common bricks will do) will be needed for the design shown here. No mortar is necessary.

It should be noted that other fuel fired kilns can be used for firing Raku. The simple gas kiln previously described would be suitable.

Firing is a skill. A remarkably small quantity of wood will be used if it is done correctly. A little fuel is added often. For a beginning, a pyrometer can be used, if one is available, to gauge how effective the stoking is. Once the technique is mastered, the eye will become accustomed to the varying conditions and temperatures, and the pyrometer should be dispensed with. Fire with an eye on the top flue. If no smoke is visible, the kiln will be oxidizing. But no climb in heat may be evident because the draught may be inducing too much cold air into the kiln. A slight smoke will show near neutralizing conditions and a rapid gain of temperature will be evident. Smoke and flame will indicate reducing conditions. Fuel is being used to no avail. Observe the ashes in the ash pit. They will also indicate the condition of the fire.

The fuel for firing should be dry, light fast firing wood. Fruit cases or long thin offcuts from a furniture factory are ideal.

Skill must be acquired in firing. Only a small amount of fuel should be used at any one time but it is not very important if too much wood is used in the early stages of the fire (to about 400 deg. C.). From here to the mature temperature of 850 to 950 deg. C. the secret is in the constant use of only two lengths of wood fed continuously into the fire box. The front part of the fire box is used to preheat the wood. The pieces of wood are spaced evenly and the fire concentrated under the fire box. As the wood is consumed at the back of the fire box the preheated fuel is fed further in. There can be no lessening of attention, this procedure is continual.

Once mastered a steady rise in kiln temperature will be attained.

For handling the ware, tongs can be improvised with a cheap pair of pincers with eighteen inches or more of light metal tubing forced on the handles. Asbestos gloves will be necessary to protect the hands, and long-sleeved clothing of a non-inflammable type should be worn. When the glaze appears to melt, the tongs can be used to remove the pieces from the kiln. Some potters judge this condition by the reflection of the tongs in the glaze. A tin of water or cold tea nearby is used to drop the ware into to cool.

A smoky reduced effect can be gained by placing the piece into a tin with sawdust or leaves in it and then covering. If copper is used with the glaze, transmutation to red can be effected.

After the kiln is emptied a new load can be immediately added. But these pots must have been well pre-heated around the top flue. They can be stacked quite carelessly one on the other in the kiln, as the glaze will still be molten when they are removed and heal over any marks. Usually about fifteen minutes will bring the glaze to maturity, if the temperature is not lost during reloading.

Colour can be obtained with oxides under, in or over the glaze. Tin will whiten the glaze. Although raw lead glazes are widely used, it is best to use fritted lead or borax glazes, as the raw lead glazes are still soluble at these temperatures.

The following are glazes which mature between 850 and 900 deg. C.

BORAX GLAZE
Borax 70 percent
Ball Clay 30 percent

LEAD/BORAX FRIT GLAZE
Lead Bisilicate 16 parts
Borax Frit 4 parts
Feldspar 2 parts
Kaolin 1 part

Some gum may be added to the glazes if necessary.
In the United States Raku firing is being extensively used to fire sculpturesque shapes. Often the kiln is built around the piece. Raku pottery is inexpensive. The materials are easily available. Yet the results have an appeal which grows.

1   The base course is laid, with the bricks on their four-and-a-half-inch side. One side is five-and-a-half bricks long, the back wall is one-and-a-half bricks long, the other side is five bricks long. The walls are nine inches apart. Normal bricklaying practice is followed. The second course is moved inwards about half an inch to support the grate.

  The grate is formed with six bricks about three inches apart to allow flow of air and fall of ash. The wall bricks are tight against the ends of the transverse bricks which form the grate.

  The next two courses of bricks are moved inwards half an inch to support the roof of the firebox and the floor of the firing chamber.

2 At the next stage nine bricks are added to form the roof of the firebox. After the sixth brick a space of two inches is left. A further space of three inches is made between the ninth brick and the rear wall. These last three bricks are, in effect, the floor of the firing chamber.
The door, which is made up of two bricks is centred in front of the three bricks which form the floor of the firing chamber. Two courses are laid around the firing chamber. A third course is moved half an inch inwards to support the roof of the firing chamber. A space of two inches by nine inches is left at the rear of the roof to form the top flue.

Kiln furniture

Shelving can be made from fire clays and coarse high alumina grog. This is satisfactory for low temperatures, but at stoneware temperatures the shelves must be of excellent quality not to warp. Silicon-carbide and sillimanite shelves are made for high temperatures. Sillimanite tends to warp after 1250 deg. C. Special kiln furniture can be bought for plates and tiles, but it is not necessary for the small potter.

Spacing props between the shelves or 'bats' as they are known, can be thrown cylinders of fireclay and grog. Ready-made spacing props are available from refractory suppliers. Firebrick can be cut. Insulating refractory brick is brittle and will not stand much weight without crumbling, but a stonemason or the refractory suppliers will cut firebricks into neat blocks.

Shelving is dusted with fine sand or silica for firing to prevent ware sticking.

A stiff mixture of sand and kaolin will make good wadding between kiln props and shelves for secure setting.

Heat measurement

Two main heat factors interest the potter. They are the rate of rise in temperature and the work it is doing. Some experienced potters fire only by the appearance of the kiln atmosphere and the ware. This takes time to learn, but once again the little Raku kiln can introduce the novice potter to judgment of maturity of ware with minor losses.

Most potters rely on some mechanical means of measuring heat. Various types of pyrometers are available which will measure the kiln temperature. Consult the supplier for advice. The pyrometer measures the rate of rise in temperatures. When firing, the rate of climb can be observed to see if the firing is being done efficiently. The pyrometer does not show the work the heat has done, only the actual heat. So if a kiln has been fired quickly, the temperature decided upon may be reached but the ware will not have reached maturity. It will show cooling temperatures, after the cones are over, where special glaze effects are required.

Pyrometric cones are the commonest means used to gauge work heat. These cones are three-sided pyramids of ceramic materials, designed to soften and bend at required temperatures. They are placed in special racks or small mounds of well grogged clay and are slightly tilted towards the direction they will fall, as indicated by the base when the cone is stood up. Three cones may be used in a kiln. The first is a warning cone, one cone number below the firing cone. When it bends, it indicates that the ware is approaching maturity. The second is the firing cone. When bent, it tells that the ware is fired to maturity. The third, or guard cone, must not fall, or the fire will have been taken beyond the point decided on. This cone is one number higher than the firing cone.

There is a small variation in temperatures relative to the speed of firing the kiln. Take care to have the cones easily seen through the spy hole. Place them in the kiln where they will give a fair idea of the average work done in the whole kiln. Special glasses, such as those used in welding, may be worn during inspection of the kiln at high temperatures.

The appearance of three pyrometric cones on completion of firing will indicate the effect of heat. In the foreground is the warning cone, in the centre the maturing cone and behind is the guard cone.

Approximate squatting temperatures Seger Cones

Seger Cone No.	Deg. C.	Deg. F.
022	600	1112
021	650	1202
020	670	1238
019	690	1274
018	710	1310
017	730	1346
016	750	1382
015a	790	1454
014a	815	1499
013a	835	1535
012a	855	1571
011a	880	1616
010a	900	1652
09a	920	1688
08a	940	1724
07a	960	1760
06a	980	1796
05a	1000	1832
04a	1020	1868
03a	1040	1904
02a	1060	1940
01a	1080	1976
1a	1100	2010
2a	1120	2048
3a	1140	2084
4a	1160	2120
5a	1180	2156
6a	1200	2192
7	1230	2246
8	1250	2282
9	1280	2336
10	1300	2372
11	1320	2408
12	1350	2462

Squatting temperatures Orton Cones

Orton Cone No.	20 Deg. C. Rise Per Hour	15 Deg. C. Rise Per Hour
022	585	605
021	595	615
020	625	650
019	630	660
018	670	720
017	720	770
016	735	795
015	770	805
014	795	830
013	825	860
012	840	875
011	875	895
010	890	905
09	930	930
08	945	950
07	975	990
06	1005	1015
05	1030	1040
04	1050	1060
03	1080	1115
02	1095	1125
01	1110	1145
1	1125	1160
2	1135	1165
3	1145	1170
4	1165	1190
5	1180	1205
6	1190	1230
7	1210	1250
8	1225	1260
9	1250	1285
10	1260	1305
11	1285	1325
12	1310	1335
13	1350	1350

appendixes

Glossary of Terms

Acid — The principal acid used in glazes is silica (SiO_2) of the RO_2 group. It is used with the bases and the neutrals to make a glaze. Borax, also an acid, gives variety of colour.

Ageing — (Weathering) the storing of clay for a period allows bacterial and chemical reactions to take place, usually in a damp, warm environment, to improve the clay body.

Alkali — Fluxing compounds: Sodium, potassium and alkaline earths such as lime and magnesia.

Ash — Ash from grasses and trees is used to make stoneware glazes. Some ashes have the ingredients, although these are not balanced, to be almost a complete glaze within themselves.

Asymmetry — Shape and form distortion, with balance usually maintained.

Bag Wall — A wall behind the firebox to prevent direct flame impingement on the ware.

Bat — A disc of material used as a base on which to throw or to dry pottery. Also a kiln shelf.

Binders — Substances used to adhere glazes to the body. Common glues such as gum arabic, gum tragacanth, dextrine and the synthetic resin range of glues.

Bisque or Biscuit — Ware fired to a hard enough body to facilitate handling in glazing.

Blowing — As the outer surface of the clay sinters during too rapid a rise in temperature in the kiln, steam trapped in the body expands and blows the ware to pieces.

Blunge — To mix clay thoroughly in a mechanical mixer.

Body — A mixture of clays and non-plastics to form a satisfactory combination for working and firing.

Burnishing — Rubbing the surface of the clay to cause the grains of clay to lie in such a fashion as to present a smooth and polished surface.

Calcine — To heat a material to sufficient temperature to drive off chemical water and remove volatile matter to render it inert; usually about red heat 600 deg. C.

Calipers — Devices to measure the inside or outside diameters of pottery.

Casting — Process of reproduction with liquid clay in Plaster of Paris or biscuit moulds.

Casting Slip — Clay which has been *deflocculated* (turned to a liquid) for casting in moulds.

Celadon Glaze — Grey-green glaze produced by iron under reduction fire.

Centring — Using the pressure of the arms and the centrifugal forces of the wheel to bring a ball of clay to the centre of the wheel. Also tapping a leather-hard piece as it rotates on the wheel to move it to the centre.

Chatter — A series of indents around a piece caused by turning a pot with a blunt or incorrectly held turning tool.

Chemical Water — (H_2O) Water chemically combined with the material being fired, which is driven off just prior to red heat.

Chuck — A clay or plaster form used on the wheel or lathe to hold pottery while turning or decorating.

Coiling — Forming pottery by the use of rolls of clay welded together.

Collaring — Closing in the rim of a cylinder with both hands while throwing.

Cones — Three sided pyramids made of ceramic materials blended in such proportions as to cause them to bend at specific temperatures in kiln firing, thus recording the work done by the heat. The two main types are Seger and Orton cones which have slightly different maturing points.

Crackle — Controlled crazing of glaze for decorative effect.

Crawling — When the glaze is fired and retracts to expose the bare body. Caused by a glaze cracking after dipping, particularly double dipping or dirty surfaces.

Crazing	(a) Cracking of the glaze caused by uneven tension between glaze and body during cooling. Sometimes long delayed. (b) The mild expansion of a porous body, through hydration causing body and glaze tension.
Crown	The roof of a kiln.
Crystal Glazes	Iron, lime, zinc and rutile with alkaline glazes will usually cause crystalline structures in the glaze with slow cooling.
Damper	A ceramic or metal plate used to control the flow of gases in a flue to give the required atmosphere in a kiln.
De-airing	Passing clay through a vacuum, while pugging, to remove all air from the clay. This process also gives instant plasticity otherwise attained by ageing.
Deflocculent	Minute quantities of sodium carbonate or sodium silicate, one third to one half percent, used to cause clay to become a liquid when mixing with the minimum addition of water.
Dehydration	Steaming or water smoking in the biscuit fire, removing water from the clay before red heat.
Devitrification	The re-crystallization in glasses and glazes in the cooling process.
Dipping	Glazing by immersion.
Dryfoot	Ware cleaned of all glaze on and slightly above the foot.
Dunting	Cracking of ware caused by too rapid cooling of the kiln.
Downdraught Kiln	A kiln built in such a way that the hot gases pass up to the crown, thence down through the ware and the floor before being exhausted.
Earthenware	Glazed porous ware fired below about 1200 deg. C.
Engobe	A coating of slip clay applied to colour or texture the body.

Eutectic	The lowest melting mixture of two or more substances: this is lower than their individual melting points.
Fettling	Finishing the leather-hard or dry clay ware by removing unwanted surface marks.
Filler	A non-plastic ingredient in clay to control shrinkage and drying.
Filter Press	A device to press excess water from clay slurry to form plastic clay.
Firebox	The chamber where the combustion of the fuel takes place in a kiln.
Firing	The burning of a kiln.
Flues	The passage ways for the hot gases in a kiln.
Flux	Any material which lowers the fusion point of any mixtures in which it is present.
Foot	The base of a pot.
Frit	Powdered material ground from specific parts of a glaze which has been melted, cooled and ground to form an ingredient in the glaze composition. Principally used to make soluble substances in the glaze insoluble.
Gel	To form a thick gelatinous mass.
Glaze	An impervious vitreous (glassy) coating on pottery.
Green Ware	Unfired pottery articles.
Grog	A ground mixture of fired clay.
Gum Tragacanth	A binder used with colour and glaze. Half an ounce is soaked in a quart of water overnight. It will then be found to be a jelly-like mass. Stir and leave all day, then stir again and it will be ready for use. Add a germicide to prevent bacteria forming.
Hard Glaze	A glaze having a high melting point because of the quantity of silica in it.

Hearth	The floor of a kiln.
Impermeable	A body vitrified to a non-porous state.
Induced Draught	Draught forced into a kiln by a fan.
Jiggering and Jollying	A method of making repetition shapes usually plates and cups on the wheel with plaster moulds and profile presses.
Kick Wheel	A throwing wheel rotated by the foot.
Kidney	A kidney shaped piece of flexible metal or rubber for finishing and smoothing clay.
Kiln	The furnace or oven for firing pottery.
Kneading	Mixing clay to a homogeneous texture by hand or foot.
Leather-hard	Partially dry clay ware, still soft enough to turn or finish but firm enough to handle without fear of distortion or damage.
Levigation	Washing with water by carrying fine particles away from coarse.
Lime Glaze	A glaze whose chief ingredient is calcium usually in the form of whiting.
Lug	Handle or knob.
Luting	Joining clay pieces with slip.
Matt Glaze	A glaze without a shiny surface.
Maturity	The point of firing when the glaze and body reach the desired state of fusion and vitrification.
Modulus of Elasticity	The ratio of stress and strain.
Muffle	An enclosed space in the kiln to prevent direct flame impingement on the ware.

Neutral Atmosphere	An atmosphere in the kiln intermediate between reducing and oxidizing.
Non-plastics	Materials which, when mixed with water, have no plasticity, such as feldspar, silica, grog and so on.
Once-fired Ware	Pottery glazed and fired in one firing.
Opacifiers	Materials added to a glaze to make it opaque.
Opening Material	Non-plastics such as silica, grog and so on used to assist drying and reduce shrinkage.
Orton Cones	Temperature cones used in the United States. The numbers do not coincide with Seger Cones.
Oxide	Any element combined with oxygen.
Oxidation or Oxidizing Fire	To fire the kiln with an oxidizing atmosphere; to have an absence of carbon monoxide and an excess of air. Sufficient oxygen will assure this condition, resulting in a clean flame without soot or smoke.
Paddling	Striking the clay form with a paddle shaped tool to thin the walls and shape the form.
Peeling	Flaking of the glaze when glaze is not under compression.
Plasticity	The condition which allows clay to be formed without cracking or crumbling.
Porcelain	Hard non-absorbent pottery, usually white or grey and translucent, fired between 1250 and 1450 deg. C.
Porosity	The quality of being able to absorb liquid into open pores.
Primary Clay	Clay decomposed from the original rock and still on the same site.

Pyrometer An instrument for measuring high temperatures, either by measuring the minute electrical charge induced into two dissimilar metals, or by optical means. Used to give the rate of rising and falling temperature. The pyrometer gives an actual heat measurement, whereas the cone gives heat work performed. As the cone is already bent after maximum temperature is reached, it cannot show the falling temperature if this is required. The pyrometer can.

Pyrometric Cones *See* cones.

Pugmill A mixer for plastic clay. The de-airing type has a vacuum chamber to remove air from the clay.

Raku Soft, heavily grogged, low fired earthenware, usually lead glazed. Today made in Japan for the tea ceremony. Raku variations are practised widely in the United States by art-potters.

Raw Glaze A glaze containing no fritted material.

Raw Glazing The glazing of unfired pottery, which is then fired only once.

Reduction Firing Firing with a limited oxygen supply so that combustion is incomplete, causing a smoky fire and flame at the ports. Normally the process is begun about the time the glaze commences fluxing. The clay and glaze are robbed of part of their oxygen content, causing changes to colour and surface, such as copper red, and celadon type glazes.

Refractory Materials having a resistance to heat, which will not melt below a very high temperature, and used for kiln building and furniture.

Rib A tool for smoothing thrown ware.

Rim The top edge of the pot.

Saggar A refractory box in which to stack ware that needs protection from the flame.

Salt Glazing	Using the vapours developed by salt when it is thrown into a hot kiln. The salt glaze covers the ware and all the inside of the kiln with a hard glassy surface.
Secondary Clay	Clay transported from its original site by water or wind and deposited elsewhere. Red clays, ball clays and fire clays.
Seger Cone	A pyramidal ceramic cone made to bend at a known temperature to record heat work performed.
Setting	Placing ware in the kiln.
Sgraffito	A decorating technique. Incising through a layer of clay slip or glaze to reveal a different colour of clay or glaze below.
Shale	Hard laminated clay.
Shard	A broken piece of pottery.
Shivering	Peeling of glaze, caused by compression of the glaze.
Shor	Non-plastic.
Shrinkage	Contraction of clay in drying and firing.
Siliceous Clay	Sandy clay or clay high in silica.
Sintering	(a) The drawing together of clay particles when fired to attain cohesion but not fusion. (b) The early maturing of a glaze.
Slake	To soak in water.
Slip	Liquid clay. A suspension of clay or glaze in water of ceramic consistency.
Slip Casting	Making pottery in moulds with deflocculated liquid clay.
Slip Glaze	A glaze made with a large percentage of clay.
Slurry	A thin mixture of clay and water.

Smoking	The slow preheating of ware in a kiln.
Soak	To hold the kiln temperature at one point for the heat to evenly saturate all the ware.
Soluble	Being capable of dissolving in water.
Stack	To load a kiln with ware.
Stamps	Pieces of wood, clay or plaster engraved with designs which are embossed on leather-hard clay.
Steaming	The slow removal of water from the clay ware in the early stages of firing before red heat.
Stilliards or Stillages	Racks to hold boards of ware.
Stoneware Pottery	Pottery which is opaque, hard and usually vitreous or non-porous, fired about 1200 deg. C.
Terra-Cotta	Low fired unglazed pottery.
Throwing	Using the momentum of the potter's wheel to draw plastic clay into various circular forms.
Transmutation	In pottery to change colours to reduction in firing.
Turning	Trimming pottery on the wheel while it is leather-hard.
Turning Tool	A tool to trim pottery on the wheel, usually a loop of wire or metal on a handle, or a sharpened edge at an angle to its handle.
Underglaze	Coloured decoration applied on the clay or biscuit ware before glazing.
Updraught Kilns	Kilns in which the hot gases pass directly from the firebox through the ware and up through the chimney flue.
Viscosity	Used in pottery to define glazes which flow slowly.
Vitreous	When pottery has fused into a non-porous, low absorbent, glassy hard mass.

Volatization	To turn from a solid to liquid to a gas in extreme heat. Particularly evident in salt glazing.
Wad	Open clay used to level shelves and seal saggars in kilns.
Water Glass	Sodium silicate. A deflocculent used in the making of casting slip.
Water Smoking	The removal of water from ware is divided into three periods. During the first, increasing heat drives mechanical water from the clay, because much remains after drying. Then hygroscopic water is removed at about 150 deg. C. Then there remains the chemically held water which is integral in the clay particles. This begins to eliminate at about 400 deg. C. and continues to about red heat. To this point the kiln should be fired slowly and carefully, with ample air passage. Once it has been reached, the rate of firing can be increased.
Wax Resist	Wax applied during decorating to prevent further application of colour or glaze on that part.
Weathering	Exposing clay to the weather to improve its plasticity.
Wedging	Cutting and striking clay forcibly to remove air and make the mass homogeneous.
Wicket	Doorway to a kiln usually constructed of loose brickwork and clammed.
Wire	Flexible wire or cord used to cut clay, or separate ware from the wheel or bat.

some raw materials and their use

Alumina	(Al_2O_3) molecular weight 101.94 is introduced to pottery through clay and feldspar. It increases refractoriness and strength of clay bodies. It is used in most glazes.
Barium Carbonate	($BaCO_3$) molecular weight 197.4, is used in glazes as a flux and to matt the surface. Some potters use barytes as a source of barium.
Bentonite	Is used as a plasticizer in clay by an addition of up to 3 percent in the clay body. In glazes, it acts as an adhesive to give stronger glaze bond and helps to prevent settling.
Borax	(Na_2O; $2B_2O_3 : 10H_2O$) molecular weight 381.43, is soluble in water. It is used as a flux in glazes, usually in a fritted form. It will alter the colour of some oxides.
Chromium Oxide	(Cr_2O_3), molecular weight 152, is used to give a green colour. Chrome turns brown in a zinc glaze. Tin tends to turn it pinkish.
Clay	is the product of decomposed feldspathic rocks. The most important clays are the kaolinite group:— ($Al_2O_3 : 2SiO_2 : 2H_2O$) and the montmorillonite group:— $(MgCa) O : Al_2O_3 : 5SiO_2 : nH_2O)$. Primary or residual clays are those found on their original site when rock is weathered into clay. One such clay is kaolin. Secondary clays such as ball clays and fire clays have been transported by water or wind. The microscopic plate-like structure of clay is thought to be responsible for its plasticity. The clay with the finest particles is the most plastic.
Clay, Ball	(Al_2C_3) : $SiO_2 : 2H_2O$) molecular weight 258, is plastic fine grained sedimentary clay. It fires white to cream in colour, usually with a vitrifying range of cone 8 to cone 10. Ball clay often has an excessive drying shrinkage causing warping and cracking when used alone. But in a body it imparts plasticity.
Clay, Bentonite	($Al_2O_3 : 4SiO_2 : 9H_2O$) is an extremely plastic clay used in small quantities to improve the workability of a clay or for the adhesion and suspension of glazes.

Clay, China	(kaolin) ($Al_2O_3 : 2SiO_2 : 2H_2O$) is residual clay of a white burnt colour because of its comparative purity. It is used in glaze to provide alumina and silica. Although not very plastic, it withstands high temperatures. It is used with a glaze to cause mattness.
Clay, Saggar	is open refractory clay, capable of repeated firings. It is used to make saggars for kilns.
Clay Slip	is liquid clay that will cover and fit the clay body, and fuse at the desired temperature to form a glass, giving a natural glaze.
Cobalt Oxide	(Co_2O_3) molecular weight 240.8, is used as a blue colouring medium. Very little is required.
Colemanite	($2CaO : 3B_2O_3 : 5H_2O$) is a natural source of borax. As it is practically insoluble, it can be used without fritting.
Copper Carbonate	($CuCO_3$) $Cu(OH)_2$ molecular weight 221.16, produces greens in oxidizing fire and reds in reducing. It is poisonous.
Copper Oxide	(CuO) molecular weight 79.6, gives green, turquoise and red.
Diatomaceous Earth	is the siliceous remains of the skeletons of *diatoms* (microscopic organisms). It is used for insulation in brick or powder form.
Dolomite	($CaCO_3 : MgCO_3$ or $CaMg(CO_3)_2$) introduces both calcium and magnesia. It is used as a flux. When added to glaze in quantity it gives interesting yellowish-tan effects.
Feldspar	(Potash Feldspar) ($K_2O : Al_2C_3 : 6SiO_2$) is the most important flux in ceramic bodies and glazes. It acts as a non-plastic opener in the clay body before firing. Feldspathic rocks are the origin of clay, which is formed by their decomposition.
Ferric Oxide	See iron oxide.

Flint	(SiO_2) is silica ground from flint pebbles. The term is also used to describe any quartz or silica sand.
Ilmenite	($TiO_2 : FeO$) is a rich, warm brown mineral sand colorant.
Iron Oxide	(Ferrous oxide) (FeO). (Ferric Oxide) (Fe_2O_3) is the most common colouring medium in stoneware giving tans and browns. When used in celadon glazes it gives greens and greenish-blues.
Kaolin	See Clay, China.
Lime	(Calcium Oxide) (CaO). Molecular weight 56, is introduced to pottery bodies and glazes as whiting (calcium carbonate) and dolomite (calcium carbonate and magnesium carbonate). Whiting is used as a flux in glaze and helps to form a hard glaze.
Magnesium Carbonate	($MgCO_3$) molecular weight 84.3, acts as a refractory at low temperature, but becomes a flux at high temperature.
Magnesium Sulphate	(Epsom Salts) ($MgSO_4$) when added to glaze in small quantities keeps it in suspension.
Manganese Oxide	(MnO_2) molecular weight 87, gives browns, purples and blacks.
Nepheline Syenite	($K_2O : 3Na_2O : 4Al_2O_3 : 9SiO_2$) is similar to feldspar but lowers the firing temperature required. Very useful in glazes and clay bodies.
Nickel Oxide	(NiO) is used to vary other colours in glazes.
Opax	is a commercial opacifier made from zircon.
Plaster of Paris	(Calcium sulphate) ($CaSO_4 : \frac{1}{2}H_2O$) is a powder for mould making.
Rutile	(TiO_2) is impure titanium oxide used to stain glazes tan and golden brown, sometimes changing to blue under reduction. It tends to matt the glaze when used in quantity.

Silica (SiO$_2$) is sand, silica, quartz and flint. In the body, it reduces drying and burning shrinkage and gives hardness and resistance to wear. As a non-plastic it aids drying, but lowers plasticity. Silica is the principal acid (RO$_2$ Group) and with fluxes it will form a glaze. In the glaze, it is the principal glass former. It will raise the fusion point and may help to cure crazing.

Silicon Carbide (SiC) molecular weight 40.07 is used to make kiln furniture. When about 0.5 percent is used with an alkaline glaze and copper, the carbon will reduce to assist in red transmutations.

Sillimanite (Al$_2$O$_3$: SiO$_2$) is used to make kiln furniture.

Sodium Uranate (Uranium Yellow) (Na$_2$O : UO$_3$) gives a yellow hue.

Talc (3MgO : 4SiO$_2$: H$_2$O) is a hydrous magnesium silicate. It is usually a white, greasy mineral, slightly plastic and in a clay body a cheap source of magnesia to act as a flux. It imparts qualities to resist thermal shock and acid attack. It is used in glazes to give a soft opaque matt surface, being viscous and stable.

Tin Oxide (Stannic Oxide) (SnO$_2$) molecular weight 150.7, is a strong opacifier. From one to two percent improves gloss and lustre of a glaze. Five to seven percent gives a white opaque glaze. Other colours are used to tint the glaze. They in turn are affected by the tin. (e.g. chrome gives pink, not green).

Titanium Dioxide (TiO$_2$) molecular weight 79.9, gives unusual matt and textured surfaces when added to a glaze. It is used as an opacifier.

Uranium Oxide (UO$_3$) molecular weight 286.14, gives yellow, brown colour. See Sodium Uranate.

Vanadium Pentoxide (V$_2$O$_5$) molecular weight 181.9, produces various grades of yellow. It burns out in reduction but will give yellow to blue-greens with cobalt oxide.

Vermiculite is used for insulation.

Volcanic Ash (Pumice) is about equal to seventy percent orthoclase feldspar and thirty percent flint, with iron content in a glaze.

Whiting (Calcium Carbonate) ($CaCO_3$) molecular weight 100.09, is used in clay bodies as a flux. But for stoneware it is mainly a glaze ingredient. See Lime.

Zinc Oxide (ZnO) molecular weight 81.38, may be used as a base or an acid in a glaze depending on the glaze constitution. An average of ten percent is common. Larger quantities of zinc cause crystalline effects in glazes. It modifies colours of other oxides.

Zirconium Oxide (ZrO_2) molecular weight 123.22, is insoluble in water. In the body zircon gives high thermal shock resistance. It can be substituted for clay, flint or feldspar in a porcelain body. It produces opacity in a glaze, needing a greater quantity than tin, usually ten percent to fifteen percent by addition. It increases hardness and stabilizes colour.

index

A
Applying colour, 77-8
Applying glazes, 83-4
Ash glazing, 86-7

B
Bag walls, 107
Bait, 86
Ball clay, 16
Bank kilns, 96
Bats, 31
Bentonite, 16
Biscuited, 82
Bowl, throwing a, 46-9
Bricks, 97
Brush glazing, 83
'Build-up' of glaze, 83

C
Calcined, 83
Calipers, 28-9
Casting slip, 16
Catenary kiln, 97, 98
Celadon glaze, 88
Centring, 33, 34
China clay, 16
Chucks, 36-7
Clay, 11-7, 76
Coiling, 59-60
Colour, 76-80, 113
Cones, 101, 117, 118
Cooling cycle, 90
Cracking, 22, 34
Crawling, 92
Crazing, 84, 92
Cylinder, handbuilding a, 68-70
Cylinder, throwing a, 40-5
Cylinder becomes a jug, 53-4

D
Decoration, 71-4, 76-91
Design, 72-4
Dip glazing, 83
Dolomite, 89
Down-draught kilns, 96, 106-8
Draping a shape, 61-3
Dry glazes, 93
Drying, 22

E
Electric potter's wheel, 26
Electricity, 96
Engobe, 77-8

F
Feldspar, 15, 16, 87-9
Fillers, 15, 16
Firebox, 107
Fire clays, 16
Firing, 85, 97, 100-1, 108-11
Flat plate, throwing a, 50-2
Flint, 16
Fluxes, 15, 16, 79
Friction wheels, 27
Frit, 78
Fuels, 96, 102-3

G
Gas kiln, 104-5
'Glaze fit', 92
Glazes, 78-9, 82-91
Glazing, 82-94
Glazing a bottle, 94
Glue, 78
Graffitto, 77
Grog, 14, 16

H
Handbuilding, 55-70
Heat measurement, 116-7
Hot spots, 97

I
Ilmenite, 76
Insulation, 99, 107, 107
Iron matt glazes, 87

K
Kaolin, 16, 87
Kaowool, 99, 106
Kick wheels, 24
Kilns, 96-117
Kiln furniture, 116
Kneading, 17, 20-1

L
Limestone glazes, 89
Liquid clay, 77

MN
Manganese, 76
Matt glazes, 90
Minerals, 77
Muffle, 97
Nepheline-syenite, 16

O
Oil fuel, 103
Opaque glazes, 90
Oxides, 76-80
Oxidizing, 77

PQ
Pinching a pot, 56-8
Plasticity, 14, 16
Plastics, 15, 16
Pouring, 83
Power wheel, 27
Pugged, 17
Pugmill, 17
Pulling a handle, 53
Pyrometers, 108, 110, 116
Pyrometric cones, 117
Quartz, 16

R
'Rag' of clay, 51, 64
Raku kiln, 96, 111-5
Raw materials and their uses, 130-4
'Raw' ware, 82

Reducing, 77
Refractory, 16, 86
Rhythm, 110
Running, 93

S
Saggars, 86, 97
Salt glaze, 85
Sand, 16
Shivering, 92
Shrinkage, 16, 22, 77
Shrinkage bar, 14
Silica, 16, 77, 88
Slip, 39, 77
Slip glazing, 83, 85
Slip on clay, 73
Slurry, 12, 69
'Spinner', 22
Squatting temperatures, Seger and Orton cones, 118
Stoneware clays, 16
Stoneware glazes, 86
Stoneware tiles, 64-5

T
Talc, 16, 89
Temmoku effects, 88
Textured tiles, 66-7
Textures applied to surfaces, 74
Throwing, 23-54
 problems, 34-5
 shapes, 40-54
 techniques, 32-4
 tools, 28-30
Turning and finishing, 36-9

UV
Underglazes, 78
Vitrify, 15
Volatilizing, 86

W
Warping, 22
Wax resist, 73, 78
Wedging, 17, 18-9
Wheels, 24-6
Whiting, 16, 89
Wood firing, 108-10
Wood kiln, 102, 108